AGING, SOCIAL INEQUALITY,
AND PUBLIC POLICY

Sociology for a New Century

A PINE FORGE PRESS SERIES

Edited by Charles Ragin, Wendy Griswold, and Larry Griffin

Sociology for a New Century brings the best current scholarship to today's students in a series of short texts authored by leaders of a new generation of social scientists. Each book addresses its subject from a comparative, historical, and global perspective, and, in doing so, connects social science to the wider concerns of students seeking to make sense of our dramatically changing world.

- *An Invitation to Environmental Sociology* Michael M. Bell

- *Global Inequalities* York Bradshaw and Michael Wallace

- *Schools and Societies* Steven Brint

- *How Societies Change* Daniel Chirot

- *Ethnicity and Race: Making Identities in a Changing World* Stephen Cornell and Douglas Hartmann

- *The Sociology of Childhood* William Corsaro

- *Cultures and Societies in a Changing World* Wendy Griswold

- *Crime and Disrepute* John Hagan

- *Gods in the Global Village: The World's Religions in Sociological Perspective* Lester R. Kurtz

- *Waves of Democracy: Social Movements and Political Change* John Markoff

- *Development and Social Change: A Global Perspective* Philip McMichael

- *Aging, Social Inequality, and Public Policy* Fred C. Pampel

- *Constructing Social Research* Charles C. Ragin

- *Women and Men at Work* Barbara Reskin and Irene Padavic

- *Cities in a World Economy* Saskia Sassen

Forthcoming:

- *Families and Public Policy* Diane Lye

Aging, Social Inequality, and Public Policy

Fred C. Pampel

University of Colorado, Boulder

PINE FORGE PRESS

Thousand Oaks ◆ *London* ◆ *New Delhi*

For information, address:

Pine Forge Press
A Sage Publications Company
2455 Teller Road
Thousand Oaks, California 91320
(805) 499-4224
E-mail: sales@pfp.sagepub.com

Sage Publications Ltd.
6 Bonhill Street
London EC2A 4PU
United Kingdom

Sage Publications India Pvt. Ltd.
M-32 Market
Greater Kailash I
New Delhi 110 048 India

Production Editor: Sanford Robinson
Production Coordinator: Windy Just
Production Assistant: Denise Santoyo
Designer: Lisa S. Mirski
Typesetter: Marion Warren
Indexer: Juniee Oneida
Print Buyer: Anna Chin

Printed in the United States of America

98 99 00 01 02 03 10 9 8 7 6 5 4 3 2 1

Library of Congress Cataloging-in-Publication Data

Pampel, Fred C.
    Aging, social inequality, and public policy / by Fred C. Pampel.
        p. cm.—(Sociology for a new century)
    Includes bibliographical references and index.
    ISBN 0-8039-9095-2 (pbk. : alk. paper)
        1. Aged—Social conditions. 2. Aged—United States—Social conditions.
    3. Aged—Government policy. 4. Aged—Government policy—United States.
    5. Old age assistance. 6. Old age assistance—United States. 7. Equality.
    8. Equality—United States. I. Title. II. Series.
    HQ1061.P323 1998
    305.26—dc21   97-45279

Contents

ABOUT THE AUTHOR

Fred C. Pampel (Ph.D., University of Illinois) is Professor of Sociology and Research Associate of the Institute of Behavioral Science at the University of Colorado, Boulder. With John Williamson, he is the author of *Age, Class, Politics, and the Welfare State* and *Old Age Security in Comparative Perspective*. He has published numerous articles on topics relating to social policy, age structure, and pension spending, and is currently doing research on age differences in income inequality and mortality from suicide and homicide.

ABOUT THE PUBLISHER

Pine Forge Press is a new educational publisher, dedicated to publishing innovative books and software throughout the social sciences. On this and any other of our publications, we welcome your comments, ideas, and suggestions. Please call or write to:

Pine Forge Press
A Sage Publications Company
2455 Teller Road
Thousand Oaks, CA 91320
(805) 499-4224

Visit our new World Wide Web site, your direct link to a multitude of on-line resources:

http://www.sagepub.com/pineforge

Foreword

Sociology for a New Century offers the best of current sociological thinking to today's students. The goal of the series is to prepare students, and
in the long run the informed public, for a world that has changed dramatically in the last three decades and one that continues to astonish.

This goal reflects important changes that have taken place in sociology. The discipline has become broader in orientation, with an ever growing interest in research that is comparative, historical, or transnational in
orientation. Sociologists are less focused on "American" society as the
pinnacle of human achievement and more sensitive to global processes
and trends. They also have become less insulated from surrounding social forces. In the 1970s and 1980s sociologists were so obsessed with constructing a science of society that they saw impenetrability as a sign of
success. Today, there is a greater effort to connect sociology to the ongo-
ing concerns and experiences of the informed public.

Each book in this series offers in some way a comparative, historical,
transnational, or global perspective to help broaden students' vision. Students need to comprehend the diversity in today's world and to understand the sources of diversity. This knowledge can challenge the limitations of conventional ways of thinking about social life. At the same time,
students need to understand that issues that may seem specifically
"American" (for example, the women's movement, an aging population
bringing a strained social security and health care system, racial conflict,
national chauvinism, and so on) are shared by many other countries.
Awareness of commonalities undercuts the tendency to view social issues and questions in narrowly American terms and encourages students
to seek out the experiences of others for the lessons they offer. Finally,
students need to grasp phenomena that transcend national boundaries—
trends and processes that are supranational (for example, environmental
degradation). Recognition of global processes stimulates student awareness of causal forces that eclipse national boundaries, economies, and
politics.

All advanced industrial countries have systems of public provision for the elderly. In the United States, for example, Social Security has been a main pillar of public policy for such a long time that the program is now considered a permanent feature of this country's social and political landscape. Not all countries have the same kind of system as the U.S. In fact, there is great variation across the advanced countries in how public old-age support operates. Some programs are very generous and shift a portion of the country's wealth from the rich to the elderly poor. Others are less generous to the elderly poor, and inequality among the elderly is greater than it is among working-age segments of the country's population. Today, the advanced industrial countries all face a growing threat to the viability of their public old-age support systems—the mushrooming population of elderly. As Fred Pampel shows in *Aging, Inequality, and Social Policy,* this threat can be addressed in a variety of ways, but each way of addressing it has different implications for inequality in the country as a whole. For example, in the United States, should Social Security be maintained at current levels, at the expense of programs for the young? Which program should be cut, health care or income maintenance? Every decision has implications that ripple through the social fabric with divergent effects not only on age groups, but also on the distribution of income and wealth across classes, genders, races, and ethnic groups.

Preface

Although students may view old age as something to worry about in 40 or 50 years, the broader topic of aging in fact relates to their everyday concerns. Students often have a personal stake in the well-being of older family members. Changes in the health and financial well-being of grandparents, parents, and other relatives as they grow older cannot help but contribute to interest in the subject of aging. Students also may realize that they have an economic stake in public policies for the elderly. Government programs invariably raise issues of fairness, and issues of fairness for one age group raise issues of fairness for others. The taxes that younger workers pay and the benefits that older retirees receive from Social Security connect the young and the old. Finally, students often have political opinions that are relevant to aging and social policy. Currently, debates over government spending, tax rates, and economic growth reveal contrasting views about policies for the elderly. Those with an interest in political and social problems should be concerned with the relationship between social policy and aging.

Despite this potential interest among students, instructors often face two sorts of problems in trying to teach them about the influence of social characteristics such as age: (a) the tendency to attribute age differences to individual physiological and psychological traits, and (b) the opposite tendency to treat social characteristics such as age as all-powerful forces that fully determine the experiences of individuals.

On one hand, students often individualize growing old on the basis of their personal experiences with elderly relatives or neighbors. Having observed changes during old age among those they know, they find it easy to view both the problems and pleasures associated with aging as personal rather than social in nature. Yet with people living longer, rates of retirement rising, and the costs for public programs for the aged growing, students need a larger perspective to help them understand the social nature of these changes.

On the other hand, students sometimes accept generalizations that implicitly treat the elderly or other groups as passively victimized by social forces. Some might perceive the elderly as victims of discrimination, prejudice, and mistreatment, whereas others might accept a contrasting view of the elderly as privileged and affluent. Yet used without care, both generalizations treat older people as essentially alike and age groups as homogenous. By neglecting the variation that exists within age-based social categories, the generalizations represent exaggerated versions of social determinism. Along with the importance of social forces of aging, students also need to understand the diversity that exists within age groups and the variety of experiences that people have during old age.

By attending to social inequality between and within age groups, I try in this book to steer between the two extremes of individualism and social determinism. Structured inequality between age groups shapes the personal experiences of individuals, but, at the same time, inequality within age groups counters simple generalizations that apply to all people of similar ages. Accordingly, aging has different meanings and consequences for people from different classes, genders, races, ethnic groups, nations, and generations. Likewise, membership in classes, genders, races, ethnic groups, nations, and generations shapes the meaning and consequences of aging. The combined study of age with other sources of inequality creates complex and diverse experiences of individuals and groups as they grow old.

The use of this theme of diversity differentiates this book from many others. Most texts on aging are encyclopedic in nature, devoting separate chapters to biology, psychology, interaction, social ties, demography, family, work, health, income, politics, death, religion, the social self, and numerous other subjects. The wealth of information and the enormous number of topics considered can overwhelm students and hide the underlying connections across topics. By presenting a more delimited perspective that emphasizes macrolevel issues, I can define a common theme that underlies and organizes the material. Although still a general treatment appropriate for undergraduate courses, the book provides a framework absent from many texts.

Several other implications follow from the book's focus on inequality. First, age inequality—more than the other sources of inequality—relates closely to government policies. Before old age and retirement, a person's income, prestige, and power depend in large part on success in the private labor market. After retirement, these factors depend more on public and private pensions than on wages and salaries. Given the shift to public income during old age, the ability of the government to counteract market-based inequality should reach its peak. Therefore, the study of aging and social inequality must include the study of public policy and its effects on the positions of age groups. I give special attention in this book to the public policies that affect the well-being of different age groups and the degree of inequality.

Second, treating aging as a source of inequality warrants the study of other societies in which both age group differences and overall inequality differ from those in the United States. Even among similar high-income, industrial, and democratic nations, many differences exist in public policy. If public policies affect the well-being of the aged, and if these policies differ across nations, then the experience of aging likewise will differ across nations. Just as aging varies by class, gender, race, and ethnic background within nations, it also varies by citizenship across nations. Thus, to help understand the larger social forces that shape old age, I make comparisons of the United States with other nations a central component of this book.

Third, the issues of inequality, public policy, and national differences spill over into topics of stratification, political sociology, and demography. The focus on inequality between and within age groups, and the combination of age with class, race, ethnic, and gender inequality, relates closely to issues of stratification. The attention to the characteristics of public programs and their consequences for inequality in the United States and other nations ties the book to topics treated in courses on political sociology. Also, the study of the consequences of population aging for public policy, the emphasis on life course change within cohorts, and the influence of generational or cohort experiences on old age all relate to topics considered in courses on population. Even more generally, the book represents an in-depth study of one social problem often treated in introductory-level courses.

To illustrate many of the concepts I review, I include numerous stories, vignettes, or narratives set off from the text and indented. These stories come primarily from published research, magazine stories, and my own acquaintances. In some cases, however, I present hypothetical cases. Michael, Frank and Vincent, Rebecca and Jennifer, Dave and Michelle, and Mary and Bill are my own creations, but they reflect realities described in the social scientific literature.

I hope that attention to diversity in the experience of aging individuals, importance of public policy, differences across nations, and links of aging to multiple topics of study help provide the tools that students need to think about social issues more generally and aging more specifically. To the extent that I succeed, I thank the coeditor of the series, Charles Ragin, and numerous anonymous reviewers for their helpful advice. I also thank the president of Pine Forge Press, Steve Rutter, for encouragement and help, Carrie Foote-Ardah and Pat Gillham for their research assistance, and the Institute for Behavioral Science at the University of Colorado, Boulder, for general research support.

Acknowledgments

Grateful acknowledgment is made to the following for permission to reproduce previously published material:

American Demographics for the paraphrase and summary on p. 72 of Langer, J., "Eight Boomers' Views," *American Demographics*, December 1995 17(12): 38-41, © 1995 *American Demographics*, Ithaca, NY.

Chicago Tribune for the paraphrase and quotation on p. 99 from Beth Ray Moseley, "Pension Sticker Shock in Europe," *Chicago Tribune*, November 23, 1993, p. N1. Copyrighted © Chicago Tribune Company. All rights reserved. Used with permission.

Newsweek for the excerpt on p. 47 from Evan Thomas, "Social Insecurity, " *Newsweek*, January 20, 1997, p. 21. Copyright © 1997, Newsweek, Inc. All rights reserved. Reprinted by permission.

Newsweek for the excerpt on p. 132 from Joe Klein, "AARP? AARGH," *Newsweek*, May 15, 1995, p. 27. Copyright © 1995, Newsweek, Inc. All rights reserved. Reprinted by permission.

People for the quotation and summary on pp. 139-140 of Dolly Langdon, "Claude Pepper," *People*, June 21, 1982, p. 38. Used by permission.

U.S. News and World Report for the paraphrase and quotation on p. 139 from Linda Lanier, "A Longtime Pensioner," *U.S. News and World Report*, August 12, 1985, p. 42. Used with permission.

1

Images of Old Age

WHEN HER HUSBAND DIED A FEW YEARS AGO, 66-year-old Martha knew she would not have to worry about finances in her old age. Thanks to the high income and wise investments of her physician husband, she owns a $450,000 house in an exclusive section of Los Angeles and can rely on income from a retirement trust supervised by her banker. Lively, healthy, and outgoing, she spends her time volunteering at the gift shop of a local hospital, socializing with friends, playing bridge, and visiting her daughters and grandchildren. She can afford to buy designer clothes, hire a cleaning woman, send out her laundry, and pay for a cellular phone in her car.

BASHA, NOW 89 YEARS OLD, lives in a one-room apartment at a Senior Citizen's Center in a deteriorating ocean-front neighborhood in Los Angeles. Despite arthritis, diabetes, and glaucoma, she must shop, cook, and dress herself; walk to and from the grocery; and travel by bus to the doctor. The need to stretch her monthly pension of several hundred dollars to cover her expenses makes these tasks all the more difficult. Having never been well-off before old age, she deals with financial difficulties the way she always has: by searching for bargains in her daily purchases. Her prime entertainment comes from sitting on a bench facing the ocean and talking with friends about children, food, health, neighbors, scandals, and managing day-to-day life (Myerhoff 1979).

TIM GREW UP IN A SMALL FARMING TOWN in southeast Iowa. After attending college, he moved to Chicago to work for a large corporation, settled in a northern suburb with his wife and children, and commuted to work in downtown Chicago. A successful career as an executive, an early retirement pension from his company, and the chance to sell his house for a substantial profit allowed Tim to retire in his early 60s. He and his wife purchased a luxurious new home built on a golf course near Tucson, Arizona. During most of the year, they spend their time golfing, exercising, socializing, taking care of daily errands, and relaxing. During the hot summer weather, they travel north to vacation and visit their children and grandchildren.

BART MOVED TO CHICAGO IN 1928, where he worked first as a clerk at Swifts, a major meat-packing company, and later as a file clerk at a large law firm. Since retirement, he has spent his days alone in his apartment. He has little money and no close friends; he never married and rarely talks to his brother in Colorado. His major activity is going to a cafeteria restaurant to eat lunch and dinner. His daily presence attracts the interest of restaurant regulars, who give him a ride home at night so he will not have to walk to his apartment through a dangerous neighborhood. A quiet and carefully dressed man, Bart keeps his distance from the regulars but depends on them as his only source of social interaction. He seems content with his life, but others feel sympathetic toward him because of his isolation and detachment (Duneier 1992).

These stories exemplify two images of the elderly in the popular consciousness. One image views the elderly as vulnerable and deserving. After decades of working, building families, and contributing to society, elderly people face limited income, poor health, and social isolation. Through no fault of their own, they may lose friends and family through death; come to depend on others for care (perhaps even have to live in a nursing home); and find themselves barely able to afford adequate food, shelter, and health care. Public policies and private efforts of family members help with these problems, but given the limited financial resources of the government and the other responsibilities of grown children, these resources fail to meet fully the needs of older people. The elderly deserve and need support beyond the levels they currently receive.

The other image views the elderly as affluent and favored. After enjoying a successful working life during a period of unprecedented economic growth, older adults have retired at increasingly younger ages with increasingly high levels of retirement income. They enjoy generous public and private pension and health benefits, leisure and recreation, and political activity and influence. Indeed, the status of the elderly has improved strikingly in comparison to younger age groups. Rather than deprived, older people appear advantaged. Government policies have attended more to this one politically powerful and affluent age group than to other, less fortunate age groups, such as children. The elderly deserve support, but not at currently generous and expensive levels.

Despite the tendency of people to overgeneralize and to embrace one image while wholly rejecting the other, both have some validity. Viewed historically, the vulnerable image better fits the experiences of the elderly in the 1950s and 1960s, and the advantaged image better fits the experiences in the 1970s and 1980s. Even within a single historical period, each fits some people more than others. The image of vulnerability applies most to the very old (who face the highest risk of poor health), widowed or divorced women who have in the past depended on the income of spouses, and minorities who have had few opportunities to accrue public and private pension benefits during their work lives. The advantaged image fits the healthiest and youngest of the elderly, married couples, and middle-class whites. Neither image, in other words, accurately portrays the lives of all older people, but both contribute to the larger picture. The validity of both implies diversity and inequality among the elderly.

The existence of varied experiences in old age defines inequality as a central topic in the study of aging. Sociologists view *social inequality* as relatively stable differences in the access of groups to valued resources such as income, power, and respect. In addition to differences in access between age groups, such as the young and old, differences exist within age groups. Aging varies across groups, societies, and periods of history, making for a variety of experiences during old age that neither of the popular images captures.

The concern with age inequality leads to some questions: How do the experiences of old age differ among subgroups of advantaged and disadvantaged elderly? What are the sources and consequences of inequality in old age? These questions raise issues addressed partly in this chapter and more generally in the rest of the book. The next sections explore the two images in more detail and draw out the implications the images have for the existence of diversity or inequality in old age. The chapter also considers the potential for further increases in inequality among the elderly in decades to come.

Improvements in the Status of the Elderly

The image of the elderly as an advantaged group has emerged in recent decades largely because of the success of public programs in raising their income. Indeed, Social Security, the main source of public pension or retirement support for the elderly in the United States, has gained a reputation as a program that works (Bernstein and Bernstein 1988). Officially,

Social Security refers to Old Age, Survivors, Disability, and Health Insurance (OASDHI). By far, the largest part of OASDHI goes to retirement benefits for the elderly, but funds also go to survivors of deceased participants and disabled people under age 65. Health insurance also goes to the elderly under the name of Medicare. In its common usage, Social Security refers to the retirement component of OASDHI.

The government also provides benefits for the more needy elderly in the form of Supplemental Security Income (SSI). Benefits from this program go to those who receive no regular Social Security benefits or who receive too little in benefits to support a decent standard of living. Those who did not contribute to the Social Security system while working and those who did not work continuously while young may fail to qualify for normal Social Security benefits. Along with food stamps, subsidized housing, and free health care, SSI benefits provide poor elderly with tolerable, if not generous, income levels.

Social Security has moved some elderly out of poverty and substantially improved the finances of many more. In 1959, 33 percent of men and 38 percent of women age 65 and over had income below the poverty line (Smolensky, Danziger, and Gottschalk 1988:33). More than one out of three elderly people did not have sufficient income to afford a minimally nutritious diet and adequate shelter and clothing, much less money for entertainment, gifts to others, and luxuries. By 1992, the percentage below poverty had fallen to 9 percent among elderly men and 16 percent among elderly women (U.S. Bureau of the Census 1992). The drop from 33 or 38 percent to 9 or 16 percent represents millions of older people spared from below-poverty income levels.

To provide a standard of comparison for these percentages, Figure 1.1 charts the trends in poverty levels for various age groups over the past few decades (U.S. Bureau of the Census 1994:476). In 1959, poverty rates for older people were higher than for children or the population as a whole, but rates for older people declined sharply during the 1970s and 1980s. By 1992, poverty among older men had fallen below the average for all ages, and poverty among older women differed only slightly from the average for all ages. In contrast, the poverty rate for children rose from 1969 to 1992. Compared to children and the total population, the elderly experienced the largest decline in poverty rates and largest improvement in economic well-being.

If anything, Figure 1.1 understates the trends. The plight of elderly people in the 1950s may have been even worse than suggested by the poverty rates, and the improvements in economic well-being even

FIGURE 1.1

Trends in Poverty Rates by Age Group

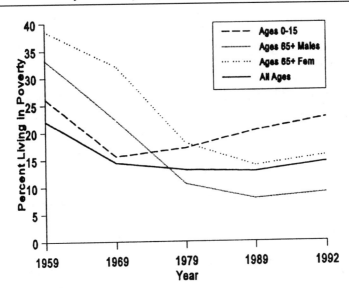

greater than shown. On one hand, the methods used to calculate the poverty line assume that older people have lower costs for food, housing,
and other necessities than do younger people. If their costs are about
the same, however, poverty rates may underestimate the percentage of
the aged population unable to meet basic needs. Although the 1959 poverty rate for those over 65 was well under 40 percent, a 1960 Senate sub-
committee reported that "at least one-half of the aged—approximately
eight million people—cannot afford today decent housing, proper nutrition, adequate medical care, preventive or acute, or necessary recreation."

On the other hand, older people may be even better off now than the
statistics indicate. Although people over age 65 receive lower cash income than people under age 65, the elderly live in smaller households,
usually without children, and therefore need to share the same income
with fewer people. The elderly usually have accumulated assets over
their lives and need to devote fewer resources to purchasing cars, furniture, housing, and expensive goods than do younger families. In fact,
older people can sell some of those assets to obtain cash income. Finally,
the elderly benefit from programs that provide services rather than cash.

Subsidized health care, for example, provides the equivalent of cash income. Thus, when adjusting for household size, assets, and noncash benefits, the average elderly person today has a standard of living at least equal to that of the average nonelderly person.

The improved financial situations of the elderly seem related to higher Social Security benefits. Michael Harrington (1962:105), in his survey of poverty in America, reported that in 1960, when the poverty level for a retired couple living in an urban area averaged $2992, average Social Security income was only $840 a year. In 1993, the average payment to retired workers was $7836 a year, just above the poverty threshold of $7809 (U.S. Bureau of the Census 1994:480). Furthermore, the percentage of elderly people eligible for benefits rose from 60 percent in 1960 to 95 percent by 1981 (Harrington 1984:225). Policymakers can take pride in these improved poverty rates. Their accomplishments seem all the more impressive given that poverty has risen among some other age groups during the same period it has declined among the elderly.

Improvements occurred not only among the poor, but also among the aged population overall (Hurd 1990). The average (both mean and median) income of the elderly rose faster than the average income of the nonelderly during the 1970s and 1980s. As a result, income of the elderly on average now equals or exceeds that for the nonelderly (Smeeding 1990:365).

In part as a result of these changes, many people can expect to experience a satisfying and comfortable old age. They can expect incomes higher than ever before, a retirement free of stress and drudgery, and many years of good health. As a group, many elderly have developed a sense of pride both in what they accomplished as adults and in the lives they now lead. Peter Laslett (1991) argues that the immense improvements in the lives of older adults have come to define a new stage of the life course. Falling between the years of work, responsibility, and saving during adulthood and the dependence and problems of late old age, the early years of old age give most people the freedom to enjoy personally fulfilling activities.

One need not look hard to notice retirees living in affluence and comfort. Homes on golf courses in Arizona and Texas, around lakes in northern Wisconsin, Michigan, Minnesota, and Arkansas, and by the ocean in Florida serve many older people quite well. Some can afford two homes, one winter and one summer, and others can afford extensive travel and recreation. Social Security benefits alone cannot support such a lifestyle, but along with pensions and savings, they contribute substantially to the well-being of a large number of middle-class retirees.

Remaining Problems for the Elderly

Despite the successes of Social Security, gaps in coverage remain. For a minority of the elderly—those with certain kinds of health problems or mental impairment, with limited savings or private pensions, and with few family members who can care for them—Social Security benefits and Supplemental Security Income fail to provide for a decent standard of living. Unfortunately, these problems often occur together, with each one making the others worse. Those elderly whose work histories limit their Social Security benefits can seldom rely on private savings or pension benefits. Those with the most serious health problems often have no spouse or family member who can care for them. People most vulnerable in one way are likely to be vulnerable in other ways.

Social policy does not deal with all groups equally well. It works best for those who conform to a certain model: people who begin work in their twenties and contribute to Social Security throughout their working lives. The contributions make them eligible for relatively high levels of benefits—not excessive or luxurious, but livable. In combination with savings, private pensions, and ownership of a home and furniture, public retirement benefits contribute substantially to a decent living standard. As long as the retirees do not develop major health problems, disabilities, or mental impairment, they can enjoy a satisfying old age.

Social Security policy works less well for those who do not fit this model. Those who do not work continuously during adulthood or do not have jobs that participate in the Social Security system receive limited benefits that barely keep recipients above the poverty line (Margolis 1990). Those with serious problems of disability, health, or mental impairment face huge expenses that can push them into destitution before they become eligible for public support. The risk a person faces during old age of becoming one of the unfortunate elderly with health and disability problems compounds the normal financial difficulties associated with retirement. Those most vulnerable to income problems when young—women, minorities, the less educated—face even more serious income problems when they become old. Public policy for the elderly in the United States does not deal with these groups and problems as well as it deals with the more typical majority of healthy, middle-class elderly people. The following example, although dated, still depicts the problems of older people outside the Social Security system.

ALTHOUGH IN THEIR 70s, Harry and Al moved like young men. Indeed, they had to be on their toes. With little money and no family, they had to hustle to survive. They had drifted across the country working at odd jobs since the Great Depression and had accumulated no savings, had no private pensions, and did not qualify for Social Security benefits. Al had been turned down for public assistance, and Harry believed he was not eligible. Having had trouble with the police over the years, they distrusted the government. Instead, they lived by panhandling, petty shoplifting, and working at odd jobs. With little income, they wore the same clothes every day and lived in a smelly, run-down hotel in a dangerous part of town. For breakfast, they walked 12 blocks in the morning to buy day-old donuts at half price. They would often try to steal food for lunch and eat it on a bench in the park. For dinner, they went to cheap cafes to order a hot meal for a few dollars. Somehow, Harry and Al managed to survive. Still, they and others like them have slipped through the cracks of the Social Security system (Curtin 1972:63-72).

The focus on statistical averages may hide the risks faced by many elderly people. Despite their decline among all older people, poverty rates remain high among many subgroups. Thirty-three percent of blacks and 22 percent of Hispanics age 65 and over remain in poverty—well above the 13 percent figure for all older people (U.S. Bureau of the Census 1994:476). Older single women also suffer more than their share of poverty. Unmarried women age 75 and over have a poverty rate of 29 percent (U.S. Bureau of the Census 1992:15). The risks faced by older women stem from the nature of Social Security, which primarily serves workers and their spouses. Although blacks, Hispanics, and older single women represent a minority of the aged population, their plight presents a more negative picture of old age than do more general statistics.

Still other people have income above the poverty level, but only barely. Moon and Ruggles (1994:210) estimate that in addition to the 4.0 million individuals age 65 and over counted as poor, another 2.3 million have income only 25 percent above the poverty threshold. Social Security benefits may push these 2.3 million people past the officially designated poverty minimum but may nevertheless leave them economically insecure. Smeeding (1990) labels this group as "tweeners," or "those caught in the middle: not well enough off to be financially secure, while not poor enough to qualify for the means-tested elderly safety net" (p. 372). Unable to qualify for social assistance, the near-poor elderly may, in fact, face greater financial insecurity than the poor. Thus, the decline in poverty rates seems less impressive than it first appears.

Furthermore, public programs may have contributed less to the improving economic status of the elderly than one might expect. Using fig-

FIGURE 1.2

Income Sources of the Elderly

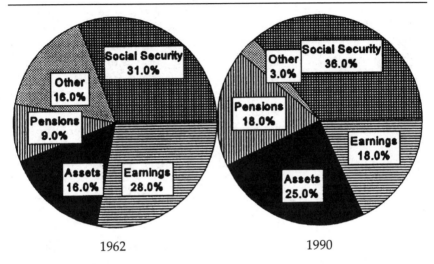

1962   1990

ures from the Social Security Administration, Moon and Ruggles (1994:213) compare the sources of income for the elderly in 1962 and 1990 (Figure 1.2). Social Security income as a percentage of all income of older people rose only 5 percent—from 31 to 36 percent. The Other category, which includes public assistance, declined substantially. Together, then, public income sources can take little credit for the improved financial status of older people. Instead, private sources of income from pensions and assets have grown the most: pensions grew from 9 to 18 percent, and asset income from 16 to 25 percent. Private income—private pension, asset, and earnings income—made up 53 percent of income in 1962 and 51 percent in 1990. The continuing importance of private income means that advantaged elderly people with public and private income sources will continue to do better than the less advantaged elderly people with public income only.

The nature of public support for the elderly illustrates both the triumph and the tragedy of old age. Public programs have improved substantially the lives of the elderly compared to 30 or 40 years ago. People look forward to a comfortable old age and a way of life unimaginable in an earlier time; they can enjoy leisure and affluence simultaneously. Yet a substantial minority suffer the tragedies of old age despite public programs. Even those who avoid poverty in old age because of Social Security benefits remain vulnerable to expensive health problems.

Changing Stereotypes

As a group, the elderly include both affluent and disadvantaged people, but it is easy to view all older people in the same way. Until recently, the elderly have been stereotyped as vulnerable and deserving: "Prior to the late 1970s the predominant stereotypes of older Americans were compassionate. Elderly people were seen as poor, frail, socially dependent, objects of discrimination, and above all deserving" (Binstock 1994:156).

The form of "compassionate ageism" contained in this stereotype has had many benefits. By combining the characteristics of both need and deservingness, the image motivated successful government efforts to improve the economic status of the elderly.

An example of an elderly person deserving of better treatment comes from a recent book on the problems of old age.

> *EVEN AFTER 71 YEARS of living in Vermont, Harold Milton finds the beauty of the changing colors of tree leaves inspiring. He has spent all his life in Vermont, and does not plan to leave now. Despite four operations (two for eye cataracts and two for cancer) and arthritis in both hands, he still works two nights a week cleaning an office to make extra money. Unfortunately, the benefits he receives from Social Security leave him below the poverty line. Even with Supplemental Security Income payments, he must live on a little over $4000 a year. After paying rent and buying some groceries, he has only a few dollars left for spending money. As a result, most weekdays he walks two miles from his rooming house to eat at the senior center for a contribution of one dollar. Harold never expected financial problems in old age. After all, he worked hard, spent wisely, and contributed to Social Security, but things didn't work out as they should have (Margolis 1990:25-26).*

If generalized to the aged population, the image becomes a stereotype that reflects compassionate ageism.

Sociological views of family life have contributed to this type of compassionate ageism. Theories dating back to the 1940s (Burgess and Locke 1945; Parsons 1943) suggested that urbanization and industrialization were disrupting extended families and isolating adult children from their elderly parents. Popular conceptions of the traditional family accepted much the same viewpoint. Compared to an idealized picture of extended families, actual family relationships in industrial cities in the United States appeared distant and detached. It seemed that nuclear families were pushing their elderly parents into retirement homes or leaving them alone and destitute to survive as best they could. This image concerned many Americans, and they began to demand that policymakers help the elderly grow old with dignity. This compassionate ageism shaped the public programs we have today. If families no longer cared for the elderly, then the government should step in to meet their needs.

However, real life seldom matched either vision of family life. The family, in fact, never offered guaranteed protection for its oldest members, and for centuries, three-generation households have constituted only a small proportion of all households in the United States and most European nations (Laslett 1971). At the same time, adult children and their parents have frequent contact and emotionally satisfying relationships even if they rarely reside in the same household or provide economic support for one another (Lye 1996). Still, the image of neglected parents encouraged action by the government on behalf of the elderly.

Some have suggested that just as racial and ethnic minorities suffer from racism, the elderly suffer from ageism, no matter how compassionate it has been (Butler 1975). Older people are assigned to subordinate positions in society on the basis of a characteristic that they have no control over and thus are victims of prejudice and discrimination. Stereotypes about the capacities, activities, and interests of older people reinforce the view that they are incapable of fending for themselves. Older adults often affirm this view by trying to conceal their age. Yet despite some similarities in the unfair treatment of older people and certain racial groups, ageism differs from racism in an important way (Binstock 1994). As a prod for government action, the image of the elderly as deprived and vulnerable has helped expand government support for the elderly and improve their economic status.

More recently, a new stereotype has emerged in reaction to compassionate ageism. It views the aged not only as affluent and advantaged relative to younger age groups, but, at the extreme, as selfish and greedy. To contrast this stereotype with compassionate ageism, Binstock (1994) uses the term "scapegoat ageism." Rather than a group in need, the elderly are seen as an elite group that can spend time traveling, golfing, and playing bridge while younger people have to work to pay Social Security benefits. An example of this viewpoint comes from a 1996 book written by Lester Thurow, a renowned economist at the Massachusetts Institute of Technology:

> A new class of people is being created. For the first time in human history, our societies will have a large group of economically inactive elderly, afflu-

ent voters who require expensive social services such as health care and who depend upon government for much of their income. They are bringing down the social welfare state, destroying government finances, and threatening the investments that all societies need to make to have a successful future. . . . Already the needs and demands of the elderly have shaken the social welfare state to its foundation, causing it for all practical purposes to grow broke. (Thurow 1996b:96-97)

The last sentence in particular seems to place the blame for many social problems directly on the shoulders of the elderly population. One can also recognize this scapegoat ageism in a story from a recent article in a well-known business magazine.

A SMALL ISLAND OFF SARASOTA on the Western shore of Florida, Longboat Key contains expensive homes surrounded by green fairways of the local golf course. James Durante, a retired lawyer from New York, owns a $400,000 condominium in Longboat Key. He and his wife enjoy a comfortable life there, as do most of the residents. The major source of conflict concerns reserving the best tee-off times on the golf course. Having worked hard in his life and made enough money to support himself in retirement, James does not need Social Security. Still, he gets a check for $1700 a month, more than most recipients who desperately need the extra income. He pays only $380 a year for Medicare Insurance, the same as other retirees with much less private income. He admits the unfairness, "I'm overpaid tremendously. In a couple of years I got back everything I ever put into the system." Although not personally selfish (James contributes time and money to several charities), the Durantes illustrate the windfall return to the well-to-do under the current system (Smith 1992:70).

Given the diversity within the aged population, the stereotype of affluence and selfishness exaggerates as much as the stereotype of destitution. Even so, the new stereotype can influence public policy in important ways. Compassionate ageism produced government action on behalf of the elderly over the past 30 years, but the very success of the efforts has produced a counterreaction. Scapegoat ageism has in turn constrained some efforts to improve public programs for the elderly, and it may well continue to do so in the future.

In summary, popular images or stereotypes can influence the meaning and experiences of old age. These socially constructed images and definitions can prove more important to the individual experiences and problems of old age than the objective facts and conditions of the elderly (Estes 1979, 1993). If older images once viewed old age as decline and decay, more recent images view old age as privileged and a burden for other age groups. Either way, dominant views tend to define the elderly as a social problem. Indeed, Estes claims that members of the aging establishment—programs, organizations, bureaucracies, interests groups, industries, and professionals that serve older people—accept and help legitimize these definitions of old age. As a result, they contribute to the socially constructed images of the elderly as a problem and help implement policies based on often misleading stereotypes.

Inequality in Old Age

The multiple images of old age highlight a crucial characteristic of the elderly population—its diversity. Although older people share similar experiences and social roles by virtue of their ages, much variation exists within these broad experiences and roles. The inequality in old age may reflect inequalities that existed before old age, or it may reflect increases or decreases from what existed before old age. Regardless, the elderly differ among themselves in the prestige, wealth, and power they have and in the way they experience the process of becoming old. This inequality in old age has become a central topic of research on aging (Calasanti 1996).

Although inequality exists in all age groups, inequality in old age has some special characteristics. For one, the elderly have had more time than other age groups for differences to emerge and accumulate over the life course. For example, few income differences would exist at age 22 between a high school dropout and a recent college graduate. The dropout might have worked for several years in a low-paying job, but would have established some seniority and received some raises. The new college graduate might also have to start out at relatively low pay. However, the potential for salary growth of the college graduate exceeds that for the high school dropout. Forty or 50 years later, the college graduate will have seen his or her income grow faster than the income of the high school dropout. Even if they begin with similar income, inequality increases as they grow older.

Given the premise that those who gain initial advantages use them to obtain more advantages, the gap between the advantaged and disadvantaged should steadily expand as a group of people born around the same time grows old. By old age, the gap should reach its maximum (Dannefer 1987; O'Rand 1996). Thus, the accumulation of advantages over the life course produces multiple and unequal pathways into old age (Henretta

1992; Kohli et al. 1991). This life course perspective considers how diverse experiences early in life produce diversity and inequality in later life (Elder and O'Rand 1995).

Another distinctive characteristic of inequality in old age is that the elderly, more than any other age group, depend on income from public and private pension programs. Compared to market income, such as wages, salaries, and investment income common before old age, public retirement income during old age may contribute to lower inequality. Although the issue remains complex, many think of government retirement programs as "fairer" and more equal than private market income. If so, the dependence of the elderly on public benefits should moderate the inequality that otherwise would occur in old age. Yet the need for such benefits in the first place highlights the potential for inequality in old age.

If the diverse images in old age illustrate the importance of inequality among the elderly, future trends warn of further growth in inequality. Despite progress in the past several decades, old age security in the future may worsen for many and exacerbate inequality.

Problems of Public Funding

Despite progress in the past several decades, old age security in the next 50 years may erode because of funding problems. The improved economic well-being of many elderly has not come without cost. Current estimates of federal expenditures for the elderly total nearly $500 million, a huge part of the government budget and a substantial part of the gross domestic product. During a period of continuing government deficits, some people question our ability to sustain these costs.

The demographic facts provide some cause for concern. Because those who will reach age 65 in the next several decades are now alive, demographers can predict with some accuracy the size of the future aged population. We know that the percentage of the population age 65 and over rose from 9.8 percent in 1970 to 12.4 percent in 1990. Rising expenditures during this time span came from both the increasingly large size of the population and from increased benefits per older person. The U.S. Bureau of the Census (1994:16), using moderate assumptions about fertility, mortality, and immigration, projects that 20.1 percent of the population will be over age 65 by the year 2030. Compared to past experience, that represents a stunning increase in the size of the aged population. Figure 1.3 depicts these changes in relation to changes in other age groups. Al-

FIGURE 1.3

Trends in Age Group Size

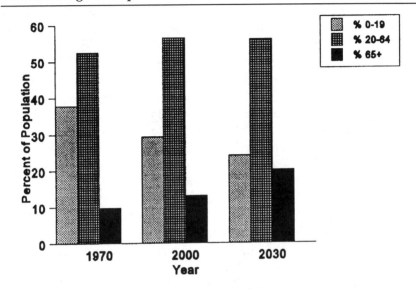

though it will remain smaller than the population of children or younger adults, the aged population will more than double, whereas the size of the other age groups will fall or remain relatively stable.

The number of older people relative to working-age adults further illustrates the importance of demographic changes. Given the structure of the Social Security system, current workers support current retirees. In the early years of Social Security, a ratio of 1 retiree per 120 workers made the system workable. By 1975, the ratio was 1 retiree per 3.3 workers, and predictions suggest a ratio of 1 retiree per 2 workers in 2030 (Kingson and Berkowitz 1993:104). The costs to each worker of supporting half of a retiree may threaten the program.

Recognizing changing future demographics, policymakers modified Social Security laws in the 1980s to deal with the potential problem. Among other changes, a 1983 amendment raised payroll taxes to the point where contributions to the system far exceeded benefits. Program administrators expect the surplus to build for the next 30 years, during which time large baby boom cohorts will reach retirement ages. By law, however, the government uses the surplus to purchase Treasury bonds, which fund deficits in general revenue spending. The bonds will need to be paid off by the taxpayers through general income taxes later on, so funding problems will not disappear.

Polls show that young workers doubt that Social Security programs will exist when they retire (Kingson and Berkowitz 1993:87). Even if the system works now, many say, it cannot continue to provide high benefits into the future. After contributing substantially during their work years and helping to support current retirees, members of the baby boom generation may have to rely more on private pensions and savings than do current or past retirees. Because private pensions depend more on previous market income than public pensions, inequality in old age will worsen for the baby boomers. Alternatively, Social Security benefits could be doled out mostly to those in need, with the affluent receiving more limited benefits. However, calculating Social Security benefits on the basis of need may reduce popular support for the program, especially among those who receive reduced benefits. Either way, changes would further aggravate the inequality in old age.

One can exaggerate the seriousness of Social Security's future funding problems. Quadagno (1996) makes the case that the facts do not justify the fears of a crisis. Contrary to impressions, spending on entitlements as a percentage of gross domestic product has grown only slightly in the past decade. Moreover, Social Security relies on the political desire of the public and politicians to meet the needs of the elderly rather than on demographic projections. If the economy grows sufficiently to substantially raise the wages of workers, the changes in demographic composition appear less threatening and the required changes in policy less severe than those suggested by the worst-case scenarios. Even so, predictions of a crisis tend to undermine confidence in the system, encourage dramatic changes in the structure of the system, and thus may contribute to greater inequality in decades to come.

Problems of Health Care

Another problem in supporting the elderly may become more serious in the future and contribute to greater inequality—the high cost of medical care for an increasingly large elderly population. Current costs of Medicare greatly exceed projections made only a decade ago, and costs will certainly grow in the future as the population of people qualifying for Medicare increases. As with public pensions, funding problems may well increase the gap between advantaged and disadvantaged groups in the aged population. Despite Medicare, those with private economic resources can afford better medical care than those without. If Medicare benefits are reduced, rates of death and sickness for high-status and low-status groups in the aged population could diverge more, and health inequalities may rise along with economic inequalities.

Public health care spending on the elderly may increase for another reason. If life expectancy continues to rise, but those last years are plagued by disease and disability, costs for health care may likewise increase. To support an increasing number of older people, public health programs must deal with the costs of treating people at increasingly older ages with increasingly more difficult health problems. These trends may, in fact, erode some of the progress made in the financial support of older people.

Changing patterns of sickness and mortality make the risks of serious—and expensive—health problems more likely than several decades ago. Historically, sickness and death came primarily from infectious viral or bacterial diseases such as influenza, pneumonia, or gastroenteritis. These acute diseases potentially affect people of all ages and do not have long-lasting physical consequences. Better nutrition, community sanitation, personal hygiene, medical treatment, and drug therapy reduce their incidence and their severity. Today, the threat comes not so much from these acute diseases as from chronic degenerative diseases involving the wearing out of the body rather than invasion by outside organisms. Heart disease, stroke, and cancer are now the major sources of death, and they strike more often as people age (Manton 1990). As a result, death and disease have become more closely associated with old age than in the past.

Another aspect of changing mortality rates may also affect disease patterns in the population. In the past, only people with particularly strong durability and resistance to diseases survived to the oldest ages. Their hardy constitution helped stave off chronic disease until death. However, improved medical care has increased the proportion of relatively less hardy people who reach old age. They may be more susceptible to disability and chronic disease than elderly people were in earlier eras. Therefore, the changing composition of the elderly population may increase the prevalence of disability and serious chronic disease.

The rising importance of disability and chronic disease has serious implications for health care. The costs of medical care for chronic degenerative diseases greatly exceed costs for infectious diseases. Surgery and critical care for heart and cancer patients; dialysis for kidney failure; eye surgery for older people with cataracts, cornea problems, or other vision difficulties; rehabilitation for broken bones; arthritis; osteoporosis; and full-time nursing care for dementia use substantial resources. The more common these diseases become among the elderly, the greater the private and public costs.

Another implication follows. If the probability of physical disease and mental incapacity increases with old age, and more and more people live to old age than in the past, then we can expect more people to suffer from these expensive chronic health problems. As the average length of life increases, people become more vulnerable to disability. People may live longer than in the past, but the quality of life of those added years may worsen. Consider the following story.

AFTER HIS WIFE DIED FROM CANCER, John wondered how he would get along on his own. Although 70 years old and retired, he was healthy and energetic—neither disability nor sickness had slowed him during old age. But he was lonely. To stay active, he moved from a house in the suburbs to an apartment in a huge "singles" complex downtown, where he met people of all ages. Surprising his grown children and grandchildren, he began dating. He said he generally enjoyed the companionship, except for some younger women who wanted to take him to the bars to drink. He enjoyed other activities. For the next 10 years, John's new life seemed to go well. However, one night not too long after his 80th birthday, he called to say that the woman who lived above him had begun harassing him. She typed all night long, made noise jumping up and down on the floor above, and slammed the elevator door on him. His complaints about the woman grew so much over the next few months that his children decided to move him to another apartment in a different building. That worked well for a few weeks, until he called again saying that the same woman had discovered his new location and moved above him just to continue harassing him. A psychiatrist diagnosed the problem as paranoia stemming from senility, but the symptoms seemed very similar to what we now call Alzheimer's disease. After a few years, his adult children put him in an expensive, clean, and comfortable nursing home. John no longer recognized his children or grandchildren, began to spew four-letter words at nurses and helpers, and had such violent rages that he once ripped a phone off the wall. He hardly seemed to be the same gentle and loving person his family had once known. Decades earlier, John probably would not have lived long enough to experience this phase later in his life, but in more recent times, such experiences have become all the more common.

Neugarten (1996) has for decades argued that the experience of old age differs among those ages 65 to 74 (the young-old), those 75 to 84 (the old-old), and those 85 and over (the oldest-old). Differences in health across these subgroups within the aged population define a central dimension of inequality. The growth of the old-old and the oldest-old relative to the young-old may worsen health problems and inequality within the aged population.

To help determine the policy implications of such trends, Crimmins, Hayward, and Saito (1994) examine the extent of physical dependency in old age. They define as dependent those elderly people in their sample who cannot provide personal care for themselves (e.g., bathe, dress, walk, get in and out of bed, go outside) or cannot manage life at home independently (e.g., prepare meals, shop for personal items, manage money, and do light housework). Roughly 20 percent of their sample of people age 70 and over fits this status. In physical terms, the other 80 percent do pretty well.

They also define a semi-independent status to include people who can provide for their own personal care and live independently but who have physical limitations affecting participation in the wider world. Another 47 percent cannot walk a quarter of a mile; use fingers to grasp, lift, or carry 10 pounds; walk up 10 steps; or stand for two hours. The remainder of the elderly population, 33 percent, have no functioning problems.

Using these definitions and their observations from their sample over a two-year period, Crimmins et al. (1994) compute the length of time that older people can expect to live in a dependent status. Their estimates show that at age 70, people can expect to live for 12.16 more years, but they will spend 2.88 years, or 24 percent of their life expectancy, in a dependent state. People at age 70 thus could expect 9.28 years free of disability, or 76 percent of life expectancy. At age 80, they will spend 43 percent of their remaining years in a dependent status and 57 percent as fully or semifunctioning. At age 90, they will spend 74 percent of their remaining years in a dependent status. Figure 1.4 illustrates these findings. People may live longer, but chronic health problems will become more likely, and they will spend more of their additional years of life as dependent.

Not all the trends in health and mortality appear negative. A more optimistic view notes the connection between improved mortality and improved health. Medical advancements in the treatment of heart disease, drug and physical therapy, and the repair of bones and joints help make older people more physically active than in years past and can add extra years of disability-free life. Furthermore, recent efforts to encourage disease prevention and healthy lifestyles may contribute substantially to a longer and more active life. Those people raised since youth to value exercise and good nutrition can reap the benefits of a healthier old age. Perhaps as a result of these trends, a recent study at Duke University

FIGURE 1.4

Age and Active Life Expectancy

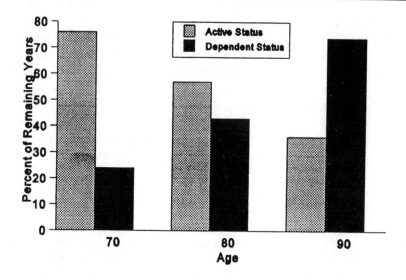

finds a decline in disability among the elderly from 1982 to 1994 (Manton, Stallard, and Corder 1995). A story illustrates that healthful behavior brings benefits in old age as well as before.

> *GAIL SHEEHY, the author of* Passages, *a best-selling book about the stages of adult life, describes how her mother's health actually improved in old age. During her 60s, her mother's lifetime of poor habits had begun to take a toll. "She always smoked, but now she chained-smoked. . . . She took up careless drinking. She ate meats drowned with sauces in death house portions." When warned about her unhealthy behavior, she said, "Don't tell me how to live my life. I don't tell you how to live yours. I have only a few years left. What I do with them is none of your affair." Just as she seemed to be bringing herself toward an early death, however, Sheehy's mother abruptly changed her habits at age 69. She started exercising and soon gave up smoking. Now 74 and feeling better than ever, she enjoys old age with energy, optimism, and good health that she could not have imagined only five years ago (Sheehy 1995:417-18).*

Basing their arguments on this logic, some scholars (e.g., Fries 1980, 1982) boldly predicted the compression of sickness, disability, and mortality into a small part of the life course. Improvements in medicine and lifestyles would postpone serious health problems until the last few years or months of life. Nearly all people would remain healthy and independent until near the maximum limit of the human life span, and then experience a quick decline and death. Although the current evidence provides little support for these claims (e.g., Himes, Preston, and Condran 1994), such compression would reduce the cost of treating the elderly.

Even with these positive developments, however, a minority may still experience disabilities and health problems. Differences between the healthy and disabled therefore may expand inequality within the elderly population. Furthermore, questions about the ability of the government to provide financially for disabled people in the future contributes to concerns that inequality among the elderly will grow over the coming decades.

A Combined View of Old Age

Although creating positive and negative images of old age has helped simplify a messy and complex social world, it has also prevented a more integrated and nuanced understanding of aging. Viewed as competing and exclusive alternatives, images of advantage and disadvantage easily become stereotypes that hide the diverse experiences of growing old. To better understand aging and the effects of aging-related social policy, we need to recognize the partial validity of both images. Aspects of affluence and destitution or health and disability not only coexist but are inherent in social and economic life in the United States.

One useful way to combine both views of old age comes from recognizing that social conditions shape the experiences of old age and the physical or biological changes that accompany them. A combined view goes beyond the usual description of differences *across* age groups to stress the variety of experiences among people *within* the same age group. The old differ from the young in their health, income, and lifestyle. Equally important, however, the experiences of aging vary substantially within old age because of the diverse social backgrounds and positions of people who share a similar chronological age and similar physical or biological characteristics. Despite similarities in physical characteristics among older people, variations in the experience of old age stem from divisions based on class, race or gender, society, and generation.

Consider briefly how these four dimensions of social life contribute to diverse experiences of old age:

Class. The experience of aging differs for people from different class or status positions in society. For example, a highly educated, middle-aged physician with high income brings many advantages into old age, whereas a factory worker with a high school degree and modest earnings will accrue fewer resources to help deal with problems during old age. The degree to which people can accumulate social and economic resources during youth and middle age may well shape the subsequent impact of old age on their lives.

Race and gender. Minority groups and females who generally occupy subordinate roles in society may face special difficulties during old age. Typically having fewer financial resources before old age, minority and female elderly people may have to deal with greater financial and health problems than do white males during old age. Age and gender or race thus combine to influence outcomes just as age and class do. Even beyond differences due to status, racial and ethnic groups maintain cultural traditions that influence the understanding of what it means to grow older and of what behaviors are appropriate for people of different ages. For example, African American, Latino, Native American, and Asian elderly people may rely more on extended family members, religious groups, and neighbors than do European Americans. Descriptions of aging particular to diverse cultures or communities can tell us much about social differences in old age.

Society. The social meaning of aging differs across societies. The status and positions accorded the elderly differ greatly in industrial societies and agricultural societies. Elderly people living in rural communities in Mexico likely have a quite different life than do elderly retired Americans nearby in Texas, Arizona, and California. In addition, the experiences of growing old likely vary even among similar industrialized and high-income nations. For example, governments in the United States and Sweden offer quite different public programs for older people. Comparisons of old age in other nations and societies can thus shed light on old age in the United States.

Generation. The meaning of aging varies across cohorts and historical periods. A birth cohort or generation—a group of people born during the same time period—experiences a world different from those born in earlier decades. Each cohort brings to old age a unique history that influences the nature of the later years of life. For example, generations that passed through their late adulthood and peak earning years during the Great Depression of the 1930s encountered a more deprived old age than did later generations that passed through late adulthood and peak earnings years during the economic boom of the 1950s and 1960s. Economic success during adulthood may coincide with success in old age. Even over the past century, then, historical change has influenced the meaning of aging for each new cohort.

Conclusion

Common images of old age—one as vulnerable and deserving, the other as affluent and advantaged—reflect complex patterns of social change. The economic lives of many elderly have improved substantially in recent decades, in large part through government efforts. They benefited from the disadvantaged image of old age, or compassionate ageism, which helped prod the government to act on behalf of the elderly and promoted public support. However, government action on behalf of older people has helped generate an advantaged image of the elderly and created some resentment over the privileges they enjoy, a stereotype that has been labeled scapegoat ageism. Scholars emphasize that problems of old age remain common among certain social groups, and that past improvements may not last without continued government efforts on behalf of the elderly. Otherwise, with the problems of population aging and increased disability on the horizon, the future may bring unwanted changes in the status of older people.

Although useful introductions to diversity in old age, the two images exaggerate and oversimplify. A more reasoned viewpoint highlights diversity. Differences in social background shape the experiences of old age and contribute to advantages for some and disadvantages for others. The physical changes of aging create the potential for high levels of inequality between the advantaged and disadvantaged, the healthy and the disabled, and the youngest old and the oldest old. Yet social forces can do much to moderate or aggravate this potential inequality. Social dimensions such as class, race and gender, society, and generation contribute to divergent experiences in old age.

The next chapters consider in more detail how social differences by class, race and gender, generation, and society affect aging. Chapter 2 sets the stage by examining how social policy in the United States contributes to inequality in old age. The next chapters consider these characteristics one by one. Chapter 3 examines how class differences before old age affect economic well-being during old age. Chapter 4 examines the effect of racial, ethnic, and gender inequality. Chapter 5 compares aging policy in the United States with policy in similarly high-income nations. Chapter 6 compares aging across generations, giving particular attention to inequity between the current elderly and the future elderly. Together, these topics explore the connections among aging, social policy, and inequality.

2

Public Policy in Old Age

IN THE WALTONS, A POPULAR TELEVISION SHOW still appearing on cable reruns, an extended family lives in the Blue Ridge Mountains of Virginia during the difficult years of the Great Depression in the 1930s. The father runs the family logging and lumber business, with the grandfather and the older children helping during busy times. The mother runs the household of 10 and manages the difficult tasks of feeding and clothing them all, with help from the grandmother and children. Supported fully by the family business, the grandfather and grandmother enjoy partial retirement, but they also contribute to caring for the children and share closely in family concerns and discussions. Even a stroke experienced by the grandmother did not disrupt permanently the three generations living together.

BEFORE SOCIAL SECURITY, those less lucky than the Walton grandparents, those without families to care for them, had few alternatives for support during old age. Even government workers had no regular retirement or pension system. John W. Perry, a postal worker, angrily discovered that an artillery horse named Rodney was retired from active duty with full support to the end of his days. "For the purpose of drawing a pension," Perry wrote, "it would have been better had I been born a horse than a human being. I have been a 'wheel horse' for the Government for the past fifty years and can not get a pension" (Fischer 1978:167).

IN 1940, the country took a crucial first step in providing for older people in a different way—Social Security paid its first check to Ida Fuller, a newly retired law firm secretary. Rather than depending on children to look after her, Ms. Fuller could support herself in part from the Social Security benefits. Although she contributed less than $100 into the program, she received more than $20,000 in benefits (more than $100,000 in today's dollars). Because she retired not long after the passage of the Social Security Act, she had little time to make contributions to the program. And because she lived to over age 100, well past average life expectancy, she received benefits for more than 35 years (Schulz 1980).

Comparing old age for the Waltons or John Perry with old age today illustrates how government programs have reshaped generational relationships. In one sense, Social Security attempts to make public the kind of private support across generations that sometimes existed within families. Younger workers contribute part of their earnings to the Social Security system, and Social Security distributes those contributions to retired people like Ida Fuller, who themselves had contributed earlier to Social Security.

Both the improvements and remaining gaps in the status of the older people described in the previous chapter reflect a long period of change in the relationship between the government and the elderly. The next section traces the emergence of public economic support for the elderly in the form of Social Security during the past 50 years. It then looks more closely at the nature of government policies today: Although social security in its broadest meaning provides economic protection to all age groups, policies offer the most generous support to the elderly. A discussion of the rules for receiving public pensions compared to the rules for receiving other public benefits suggests reasons for the growth of programs for older people. Finally, the chapter considers competing political views about the success and failure of public policies for the elderly and about the need for future changes in the program.

Government Social Protection

A negative and limited view of the welfare state raises images of government handouts for those too lazy to work. Such a view has little to do with the reality of government programs. The essence of the modern welfare state is social protection. The government uses taxes to protect or provide benefits for those temporarily unable to work or support themselves. Although not limited to old age and retirement, social protection for the elderly nicely illustrates the logic behind many government programs.

The Logic of Social Protection

In the past, children and relatives have, under ideal circumstances, supported parents who could not provide for themselves or wanted to retire. Support for the elderly traditionally took the form of an informal contract across generations. As parents cared for them as children, adult children should care for their older parents in return. This informal contract stemmed from close family ties and community norms for the roles of parents, children, and relatives.

However, adult children might not live up to the norm of taking care of older parents. They might not have enough money to support parents, they might not get along with older parents, or they might think they have problems enough without having to take care of additional dependents. As a result, protection within the family was less common than the nostalgic vision of the traditional extended family might suggest. Older people could find themselves destitute and forced to live in public homes for the poor.

With industrialization and demographic change, the family became an even less reliable source of support. As fertility declined and families became smaller, older parents found they had fewer adult children to support them. As mortality declined, older people lived longer and required support for more years than in the past. As the economy industrialized and workers moved to where new jobs and businesses were located, older parents found themselves separated geographically from relatives who could support them. As the size of work organizations increased and formal rules for retirement developed, older people found few chances for continued work in old age. Although this description oversimplifies complex processes of change (Laslett 1976), the changes exacerbated problems of traditional forms of social security (Cowgill 1986).

In modern societies, the state or government came to play a dominant role in providing economic support for the elderly. Laws required that workers set aside part of their earnings as contributions to support those who could not work. The system represents a form of forced saving, except that the money goes to current retirees rather than to a retirement savings account waiting for the contributors. The system therefore does not rely on the ability of individuals to plan for themselves, but still offers a form of protection for older people when they can no longer support themselves.

Such programs for retirement also represent a form of shared social protection. By requiring most workers to participate in the program, the government creates a massive insurance pool. Some workers may never need benefits because they work nearly all their lives; other workers may receive benefits that exceed the value of their contributions. Despite unpredictable needs for any one individual, the average risks for a large group of workers are more predictable. Like a life insurance program, Social Security shares risks across the population, but, unlike a life insurance program, those who live longer get more benefits.

A Brief History

Public policies to support the elderly first emerged in European nations during the late nineteenth century. In 1881, the famous German chancellor Otto von Bismarck launched an old-age social insurance program for workers. Bismarck hoped that state-sponsored pensions would make workers loyal to the Prussian monarchy. He also hoped to use the program as a means to resist potentially more radical socialist programs (Rimlinger 1971). As a result of these forces, social insurance emerged in Germany earlier than in most other countries. Other European nations followed with their own programs in the next several decades.

The United States began to offer pensions to Civil War veterans and social assistance benefits to widowed mothers during the late 1800s and early 1900s, but it did not develop a full-fledged insurance program until much later than most nations (Skocpol 1992). Like workers at younger ages, most older people experienced rising income during this period of industrial growth (Haber and Gratton 1994). Pockets of poverty existed among minorities, immigrants, and older women without family, much as they do today, but little pressure came from the majority of the population to enact more comprehensive forms of social insurance such as existed in Germany or Britain.

The Great Depression in the 1930s provided the stimulus for the passage of Social Security. Extremely high rates of unemployment and the crash of the stock market wiped out private sources of support for many older people. During these years of high unemployment, the elderly could not find jobs, lost savings invested in businesses and banks, and received little in the way of public or private pension benefits. Because of similar economic difficulties, families likewise could not support their elderly members. As illustrated by the story of the Townsend movement, these problems generated a great deal of social and political discontent.

FRANCIS TOWNSEND, a tall and gaunt man in his 60s at the time of the Great Depression, became a popular representative of those concerned about the problems of poverty among the elderly and the need for public pensions. Although trained as a physician, Townsend moved to California in the 1920s where he invested in real estate. The collapse of the California economy and real estate market in the 1930s was a financial disaster for Townsend. Unlike many others, however, he was able to find a job as a physician in the health department. There he observed the misery brought about by the Depression

firsthand: "I stepped into such distress, pain, and horror; such sobbing loy-
alties under the worst possible circumstances as to shake me even today with
their memory." After losing his own job, he proposed in a letter to a newspa-
per an old age pension plan of giving $150 a month for everyone over age
sixty. The idea soon became widely popular. Within the next few years, Town-
send became the leader of a national crusade with perhaps 3.5 million follow-
ers. Although Congress did not adopt Townsend's proposal, his movement
convinced many legislators of the need to address with other legislation the
plight of the elderly (Fischer 1978:182-84).

Eventually, Social Security legislation passed in 1935, and Ida Fuller received the first check in 1940 (Berkowitz and McQuaid 1992).

Since then, Social Security benefits have evolved from supplements to
savings and private pensions to the largest source of support for most
elderly. Social Security benefits and Social Security coverage improved
slowly during the 1950s and 1960s but still remained meager. The high
rates of poverty among the elderly in those years reflected the low levels
of support. By the late 1960s and 1970s, benefits began to improve. In the
1960s came the passage of Medicare—universal health care for the elderly—and in the 1970s came automatic yearly increases in Social Security benefits to keep pace with inflation. Benefits continued to grow, although not as quickly, during the 1980s. Few other programs kept pace
with the improvements enjoyed by the elderly.

Besides providing increased economic support, the government came
to also define the timing and meaning of old age (Kohli et al. 1991). With
laws and regulations that define the ages of eligibility for public benefits,
programs help define the ages at which old age begins. The ages of eligibility reflect commonly held beliefs about the approximate ages when
people can or should retire. Yet by defining the transition in terms of a
single year, the government gives concrete and precise meaning to the
more general and flexible social conceptions.

The legally defined ages of retirement have come to take on particular
importance in social life. People come to judge their own behavior and
the behavior of others on the basis of their calendar or chronological age
and the legally defined retirement ages. Individuals are defined as old
not by their behavior but by their chronological age (Neugarten 1996;
Riley, Kahn, and Foner 1994). Even the idea of old age as a period of life
beginning at age 62 or 65 in which workers can withdraw from the labor
force and enjoy leisure without a substantial drop in their standard of
living emerged in part from the rules defined by government policies.

A Welfare State for the Elderly

The need to support older people would seem obvious given their withdrawal from work in the form of retirement. Indeed, in the United States, Social Security refers to a set of programs, including old age, survivors, disability, and health insurance, that is directed toward the elderly and their dependents. Social Security has become synonymous with old age and public retirement pensions. Yet this particular usage of the term differs from usage in other countries and illustrates the important role of the elderly in public programs.

The Meaning of Social Security

In principle, social security has a broad meaning. It refers to a wider variety of programs than those aimed at the elderly. More generally, the term "social security" refers to programs established by governments to protect individuals against interruptions or loss of earning power, and for certain special needs arising from marriage, birth, or death (Social Security Administration 1985). In other words, circumstances besides old age may lead to loss of income and a reduced standard of living. Social security programs help protect people from these risks.

Consider some examples of social security programs. Workers face loss of earning power from involuntary loss of work because of unemployment. People laid off from their jobs because of an economic recession or low demand for the kind of work they do face periods without income through no fault of their own. Unemployment insurance provides short-term benefits for people while they look for another job and reenter the labor market. Similarly, a person who breaks his leg on the job or must receive chemotherapy for cancer cannot work. Worse, the high cost of medical care to deal with the health problems would aggravate income problems. Benefits for disability, occupational injury, and long periods of sickness help protect workers from these risks, and government health care programs protect people from the high cost of medical care.

Other programs fall under this broad definition of social security. In many countries, governments contribute money directly to families who raise children. Families with children under ages 16 or 18 get regular payments from the government to help support the children. These payments, called family or child allowances, are meant to supplement wages of working parents. Because those raising children face greater expenses than do those not raising children, governments help with these additional expenses to maintain the standard of living during the normal process of family building. Other programs provide assistance only to families without two parents or with especially low incomes, but also direct benefits toward the raising of children.

In many ways, then, all of us face certain risks in today's world. These risks seem greatest in old age but also affect people at other ages. The example below illustrates the general nature of social security and its relevance to people of all ages.

WHEN ASKED, Michael said that neither he nor his parents had ever been on welfare. With welfare defined narrowly as social assistance to the poor, he is right. But when asked about other programs not typically defined as welfare, he realizes the large role of the government in his life and his parents. Now enrolled in college, Michael relies in part on loans for tuition, room, and board. By agreeing to pay off his loans if he does not pay them off himself, the government makes it possible for a student without any assets to get a loan. Michael's father can help pay for college costs also. A veteran of the Vietnam war, Michael's father went to college with funding from GI benefits. The college education supported by the government got him a well-paying job and allows him to help Michael. Even a short period of unemployment did not harm Michael's family's economic status too much, because unemployment benefits kept food on the table while his father looked for work. Michael's grandmother has had serious health problems lately, but fortunately, Medicare pays for most of the hospital and physician bills, and she can live off of her Social Security benefits. Otherwise, Michael's father would have to pay for her care instead of for Michael's college. Neither Michael nor anyone in his family has received public assistance for the poor, but all have received the benefits of the more general social protection program.

Of course, old age fits this wide conception of social protection too. Old age involves both increased risk of loss of earnings through retirement and poor health, and high health care costs. Thus, benefits available to the elderly help deal with these risks but, at least in principle, represent only one part of larger efforts of social protection.

Governments provide for more than social security alone. The welfare state consists of many public institutions designed to maintain decent living conditions for its citizens (Palme 1990). In addition to social security, the broader welfare state supports education; retraining of workers; public sector employment; and subsidies for food, housing, and energy. The welfare state also protects its citizens with laws and regulations concerning employment, the environment, consumer purchases, and discrimination. All such efforts reduce the reliance of individuals on work in the private labor market as the primary source of economic support (Stephens 1986).

Given the variety of risks of economic insecurity, providing for social security remains a central goal of governments. In a market economy, loss of earnings from health problems, old age, or unemployment remains a possibility for nearly all workers. The labor market cannot guarantee earnings for all individuals; risks of loss of jobs remain ever present. At the same time, the risks are uncertain enough that few people would save for them on their own. As people view their situation in the short term, they fail to foresee problems in earning power that might occur in the future. The government, through a variety of types of programs, provides a means to share these risks.

Support for the Elderly in the United States

In practice, however, support for the elderly by the welfare state exceeds that for other groups. Consider first the public sources of support for the elderly in the United States. The largest program, Social Security retirement benefits, goes to people who contributed to the system for up to 10 years. (Rules of eligibility are actually more complex: Workers need to contribute for 3 months per year during their working lives, but no more than 40 quarters or roughly 10 years.) They then become eligible for benefits at age 65 or for reduced early retirement benefits at age 62 (this age of retirement will slowly rise in the next two decades in order to help reduce costs). More than 90 percent of retired workers and couples age 65 or over receive Social Security benefits (Quinn and Burkhauser 1990). Those eligible for Social Security retirement benefits also become eligible for Medicare, which partially covers costs for physician and hospital care. Finally, elderly people who do not receive Social Security benefits (or at least not enough to live on) can receive Supplemental Security Income. These benefits depend on need rather than on contributions, but they are designated specifically for older people.

The elderly also receive government support through a variety of tax benefits. Without going into the complexities of the tax system, a list of tax benefits for the elderly includes the following: (a) People over age 65 can reduce their taxable income and in some cases receive tax credits; (b) people with income under a specified amount do not pay taxes on their Social Security benefits; (c) homeowners over age 54 can sell their principal residence without paying taxes on the additional value the home gained over time; (d) workers can defer taxes paid into private pensions during working years and can also defer taxes on the interest on those contributions until old age. Although not huge, tax benefits nevertheless represent another source of government support.

The elderly can also qualify for benefits available to people of all ages. Food stamps, housing subsidies, and free food often go to the elderly. For those elderly people with special health problems, Medicaid provides long-term care benefits. Medicaid benefits provide health care to the poor of all ages, whereas Medicare goes to the elderly alone. Yet 45 percent of Medicaid costs in 1988 went toward nursing home and long-term care (Kingson and Berkowitz 1993:157). Although some younger people require long-term care, the need becomes greater at older ages. Thus, many elderly who cannot pay for such expensive care rely on Medicaid for support.

The government also supports people of all ages with disability insurance, but the probability of disability increases with age. Strictly speaking, this program does not benefit the elderly because at age 65, disabled people begin receiving Social Security benefits instead of disability benefits. Nevertheless, most recipients are close to old age, and disability may be seen as a form of early retirement for those who experience health problems before the traditional retirement age.

The importance of the elderly in government programs shows in spending levels. Figures from the 1997 federal budget disclose that 39 cents of every dollar spent by the federal government goes to the programs for the elderly—Social Security, federal retirement programs, and Medicare (Thomma 1997). Two other programs that benefit people of all ages—Medicaid and low-income assistance—take up another 12 cents of every federal dollar spent. Programs for education, veterans, and unemployment cost only 6 cents. By comparison, 16 cents of every dollar goes to defense, 15 cents to paying interest on the federal debt, and 8 cents to everything else (e.g., parks, foreign aid, agriculture, and law enforcement). In total dollar amounts, Social Security and Medicare cost the federal government $562 million.

Figure 2.1 further illustrates age-based trends in spending (U.S. Bureau of the Census 1994:370). To show the rise in Social Security and Medicare spending, the figure displays two lines: one for Social Security and Medicare spending as a percentage of total government spending, and one for Social Security and Medicare spending as a percentage of civilian government spending (i.e., total government spending minus spending for national defense). Both measures rise substantially. Beginning at near zero in 1940, Social Security and Medicare spending reach 63

FIGURE 2.1

Social Security and Medicare Spending

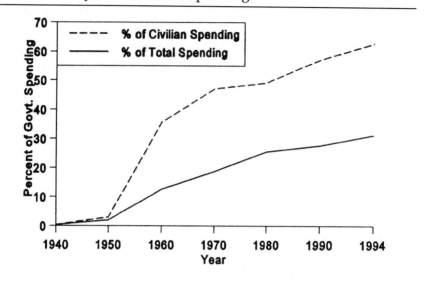

percent of civilian spending and 31 percent of total spending by 1994. Having risen faster than any other program of similar size, spending for these two programs now comprises a huge part of the federal budget.

Support for Other Age Groups

Public support for children in the United States takes a different form. Outside of schools, governments contribute to raising children through benefits for poor families and tax deductions for others. Aid to Families with Dependent Children (AFDC), the most well-known welfare program for children in the United States, has supported single-parent families with below-poverty or close to below-poverty income. In 1997, federal legislation replaced AFDC with Temporary Assistance to Needy Families (TANF). The new program still offers benefits to the most needy, but it has a limit of five years and requires recipients to become involved in a work program within two years. Other programs for those in need, such as food stamps, subsidized housing, and health care, also help poor children.

Tax deductions can also help with the cost of raising children. Like tax deductions for the elderly, a tax deduction of $2450 in 1994 for each child reduces taxable income (legislation in 1997 raises the deduction for middle-income families). The ultimate dollar benefit depends on the tax rate on that income. To this extent, parents with the highest incomes, who pay the highest taxes, benefit most from the tax deduction. The poor, who pay little in the way of taxes, get little return from children in the tax code.

The major source of support of children comes from educational expenditures. Yet educational expenditures, although important to society and families, reflect a different logic of social protection than do other welfare state programs (Wilensky 1975). Rather than social protection, educational spending seems more like an investment in future earnings. Furthermore, most funds for schooling go to teachers and employees rather than directly to students. The educational system functions more as a training system than as a social security system. Therefore, scholars typically treat educational expenditures as separate and different from social security programs.

Overall, programs for children comparable to insurance programs for older people do not exist in the United States. Except in cases of extreme poverty, the family is expected to provide for its own children. In contrast to the United States, however, all other high-income nations offer universal benefits to children similar to old-age benefits in the form of family or children allowances (Kamerman and Kahn 1988). Receipt of family allowance benefits does not depend on income or financial need. Despite some calls for such a program, the United States does not provide family allowances.

Government also plays a relatively small role in the lives of adult citizens in the United States. Adults can gain short-term unemployment or medical and disability benefits if they demonstrate need. Yet the government does not generally make cash benefits or services available to people on the basis of age for those who are neither young nor old. Except for brief periods of difficulty, able-bodied people not caring for children are expected to support themselves. What efforts governments do make for adults is to contribute to the full functioning of the labor market. Government policies may support the creation of new jobs so that adults can support themselves. Official policy in the United States calls for full employment, but few actual job creation programs are in force in the United States. Other nations have made greater efforts to keep unemployment low as a means to support adults.

To illustrate differences in age-based public programs, Figure 2.2 compares spending for the elderly to spending for other groups in the United States. Although available for a shorter time span than federal spending on Social Security and Medicare, spending figures for federal, state, and local social welfare appear in the Statistical Abstract for 1970,

1980, and 1990 (U.S. Bureau of the Census 1994:370). These figures allow one to separate social welfare spending on old age (i.e., for Social Security, Medicare, Supplemental Security Income, veteran's pensions, and institutional care) from social spending on education and other programs. Figure 2.2 presents the changes with a bar chart. As a percentage of all social spending, programs for older adults have risen substantially, whereas education and other programs have fallen sometime during the past 20 years.

In summary, the United States offers relatively large and generous social insurance programs for retirees. Except for short-term unemployment insurance or disability, similar programs do not exist for children and adults. Means-tested programs for the poor and tax deductions for the affluent do exist, but these go to older adults as well as to younger people. Consequently, poverty has fallen more for the elderly than the nonelderly, and public programs play a central role in the improved well-being of many people in recent decades.

Support for Public Programs

Why do differences exist in the levels of spending for different age groups? Because both children and the elderly are vulnerable and deserving groups, we might expect similar public programs for them. One might answer that we view raising children as the duty of parents and view taking care of older parents as the duty of the government. Although that might explain why government spending is higher for the elderly, it does not tell us why we view one task as suitable for the government, but not the other. Perhaps differences in the types of programs for children and the elderly contribute to the differences in spending.

Social Insurance and Means Testing

The spending levels of programs for the elderly relative to other age groups stem in part from the form each type of program takes. Although they overlap to some degree, two types of programs dominate social policy in the United States. *Social insurance* programs distribute benefits on the basis of contributions made into an insurance system. They gain the most popular support and offer the most generous benefits. *Means-tested* programs distribute benefits on the basis of low income, high need, and

FIGURE 2.2

Public Spending on Age Groups

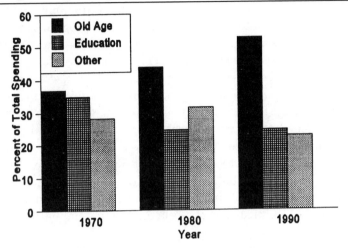

limited means of personal support. They gain less popular support and offer lower benefits (Marmor, Mashaw, and Harvey 1990).

Social insurance programs determine eligibility for benefits from con-tributions made during periods of employment. People who contribute to the public insurance pool while working gain the right to receive bene-fits later on. For example, those who contribute to Social Security for ap-proximately 10 years become eligible for benefits when they reach retire-ment age; or if they become disabled before retirement age, they can obtain disability benefits. Generally, the level of benefits received de-pends on the contributions made. In this sense, social insurance benefits reflect earnings and status in the labor force: Those who earn the most while working and contribute the most in taxes get the most benefits back.

Means-tested programs provide benefits by comparing resources against a standard based on subsistence needs. Typically called welfare in the United States and social assistance more generally, they target their benefits for the most needy, usually those otherwise uncovered by social insurance programs. Many people with low earnings fail to contribute sufficiently to insurance systems to qualify for benefits. Aid to Families with Dependent Children and, more recently, Temporary Assistance to Needy Families represent the most well-known means-tested program, but Supplemental Security Income (SSI) for the elderly takes the same form. Titmuss (1974) termed these programs "residual" because the government assumes responsibility only for those who do not or cannot participate in the market-based insurance programs for social protection.

Although the United States has both types of programs, the largest, most popular, and best funded are social insurance programs for the elderly. There are several reasons for this. First, social insurance programs strengthen ties across generations where means-tested programs promote divisiveness. Social insurance programs help link workers and retirees together in generational sharing. Workers support retirees in the present in exchange for the support new workers will give to them in the future as retirees. Both current retirees and current workers come to have a stake in keeping the system going. Means-tested programs, in contrast, highlight the gap between those who cannot support themselves and others who can. Most contributors feel, rightly or wrongly, that they will never need means-tested benefits. Rather than forming bonds between contributors and recipients, means-tested programs emphasize their differences.

Second, most citizens view social insurance benefits as a deserved reward and means-tested benefits as a handout. Because social insurance benefits stem from earlier contributions, it seems only fair that individuals get back what they put in. After contributing to the system over decades of work, retirees view leisure as a deserved reward. People tend to view means-tested benefits as less deserved. Although many understand the need for short-term help for those facing a financial crisis, they generally will not support generous benefits. They fear that providing unearned benefits may discourage efforts of people to support themselves. Instead, much effort goes into ensuring that people who receive benefits do not have too much money from other sources.

Third, social insurance benefits go primarily to the vast middle class rather than to the poor. Social insurance programs thus gain support from the large, economically more successful, and politically more powerful middle and upper-middle segments of the stratification system. Means-tested programs go toward the smaller, less economically successful, and politically weaker poor and minority groups. In one sense, means-tested programs go to those most in need and thereby may effectively redistribute income from the well-off to the poor. Yet given that relatively small and less powerful groups benefit from such redistribution, these programs gain limited public support.

Fourth, social insurance programs help unify recipients and clients to act together on behalf of the program. The links across generations and the connections across groups within the aged population represent a political and social resource. People who otherwise differ in social positions and background come to have common interests in government programs. These common interests in turn create widespread support for social movements aimed at expanding or protecting benefits of the programs in which they participate. These types of resources prove crucial for the success of social movements in reaching their goals. In the end, social insurance programs directed to large segments of the population unify beneficiaries in ways that increase their social and political resources, and thereby further strengthen the program and generosity of the benefits.

As a result of this political logic, people prove much more willing to pay for social insurance programs such as Social Security than for means-tested programs. The General Social Surveys for the years 1983 to 1993 asked respondents if they thought that the levels of spending for a variety of government programs were too high, about right, or too little. Figures 2.3a and 2.3b present the percentages of each response for two types of programs—Social Security and welfare. Only 6.2 percent of respondents thought that the government spent too much on Social Security, but 45.4 percent of respondents thought that the government spent too much on welfare. Based on these results, it is not surprising that spending for social insurance-based retirement programs greatly exceeds that for means-tested programs for other age groups. In the words of Wilbur Cohen (Cohen and Friedman 1972), "A program that deals only with the poor will end up being a poor program" (p. 12).

A European Perspective

Many European nations take an approach to social protection that differs from both the social insurance and means-tested programs in the United States. In Sweden, for example, the government offers benefits on the basis of citizenship rather than on the basis of contribution or need (Esping-Andersen 1990). Qualification for benefits does not rely on past work history, contributions, or income levels. Universal health care makes medical services available to all citizens; universal pension benefits go to all people beyond a specified age, such as 65; family allowances provide benefits to all families with children under a specified age, such as 18; and unemployment or disability benefits go to those who cannot work.

Some argue that programs based on citizenship rights promote even more popular support than social insurance. Despite their general popularity, social insurance programs tend to divide mainstream workers

FIGURE 2.3

Support for Social Security Spending

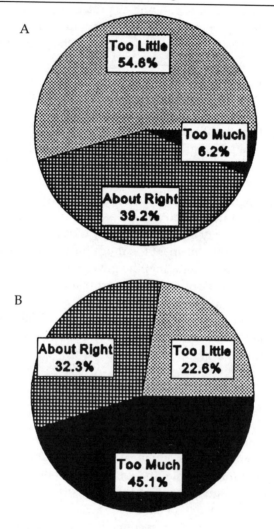

from those who do not qualify. A gap emerges between the "haves" and "have-nots." In contrast, universal systems create equality. They gain support from all segments of the stratification system and unite rather than divide citizens.

Another source of support for universal programs comes from the high levels of protection they provide from the risks of the labor market. Esping-Andersen (1990) argues that social protection does not become complete until the government offers means of economic support unrelated to market work. Because means-tested benefits are kept low to encourage people to work, they fail to free individuals from the demands of the labor market. Because social insurance benefits rely on previous work-based contributions to define the right to current benefits, they maintain links to the market. A complete welfare state, fully based on citizenship rights, would protect workers altogether from having to depend on the market for economic support.

Compared to social insurance systems, universal systems offer more complete protection for one group at high risk of poverty in old age—widowed and divorced women. Gender represents a major source of inequality in old age because social insurance programs do not provide for people—nearly all women—who spend most of their adult years caring for children and performing household tasks rather than working in the paid labor force. Nonworking women (and, less commonly, nonworking men) can qualify for Social Security benefits through the earnings of their spouse. Yet benefits earned through others do not provide the same degree of protection as the workers themselves get. Receipt of universal benefits, in contrast, does not require employment and therefore does more to protect women from financial problems during old age.

According to Esping-Anderson (1989), emphasizing citizen rights in universalistic programs means that

> citizens can freely, and without potential losses of job, income or general welfare, opt out of work under conditions when they, themselves consider it necessary for reasons of health, family, age or even educational self-improvement; when, in short, they deem it necessary for participating in the social community. (p. 22)

Few, if any, nations meet the high standards of citizenship rights defined by this statement. Despite the high public support for such programs, political debate exists in all nations over how much governments should spend on expensive citizenship-based programs. Advocates note the benefits of equality and high levels of popular support; opponents emphasize the high taxes and loss of market efficiency in such programs. Debates over the appropriate role of the government and market in social security translate into debates over the nature of successful programs.

Sources of Inequality

At the same time social insurance policies contribute to the improved economic well-being of the elderly, they also contribute to inequality. Indeed, the very nature of the social insurance programs that produce affluence among some segments of the elderly population also leaves others less well-protected. By linking benefits to contributions, a social insurance system gains a reputation for fairness—people get what they put in. Yet it also neglects those who remain relatively unattached to the labor force during the adult years. In contrast to Sweden, Denmark, and the Netherlands, where universal benefits unite all elderly, the United States relies on dual systems: social insurance benefits for those who contribute sufficiently to the system and means-tested benefits for those who do not.

As a result of the dual system of public support, the elderly in the United States inhabit two worlds that correspond to the popular images of old age (Crystal 1982). The first world includes younger, married, white, and healthy elderly people who receive the lion's share of Social Security benefits and have private income to extend public benefits. The second world includes older, female, unmarried, and minority older people in poor health with little income overall. They qualify less often for social insurance-type benefits, rarely have substantial pension or savings, and must depend on means-tested programs.

These two worlds of aging go back at least several decades. Two books about old age written in the 1970s present starkly contrasting pictures. Garson Kanin (1978), a well-known screenwriter and director, writes of Dr. Gustav Eckstein in his book, *It Takes a Long Time to Become Young*:

> ALTHOUGH 88 YEARS OLD, Dr. Eckstein continues to write, teach, and see patients at the College of Medicine of the University of Cincinnati. For 60 years, he has been one of the most popular teachers at the University and has been allowed to stay well past normal retirement age. He continues to tirelessly pursue his work and his hobbies. Besides having lived in Japan and France, he travels to Russia nearly every year to do research on the famous psychologist Ivan Pavlov, and he has begun to learn Russian. He has written several books on nature, a few plays, and a successful novel. Kanin views him as "living proof that it is not activity that wears out the human machine and spirit, but inactivity" (p. 91). Still, a successful career as a professional, good health, and high income have also helped Dr. Eckstein enjoy old age. He inhabits the more advantaged world of old age.

A few years earlier, Sharon R. Curtin wrote a much more pessimistic book about the lives of elderly people inhabiting the less advantaged world. In *Nobody Ever Died of Old Age*, she describes the life of Letty:

> LIKE OTHER OLDER WOMEN found on the streets of most any large city, Letty carried all her belongings in two shopping bags wherever she went. She

could not leave her possessions in the cheap hotel rooms she rented because they would be stolen from her room while she was gone. Worse, she worried about junkies who, learning of her routine, would rob her of her welfare checks. She did not want to spend much time at the hotels anyway. The rooms typically contained only a simple cot and chair, were infested with cockroaches and rats, and had not been cleaned in years. She often spends much of the day standing in line for Medicaid and food stamp benefits. She had to be tough to survive this life, and did the best she could under the circumstances (Curtin 1972:85-91).

Both then and now, the existence of the two worlds of aging results in part from public policy. Along with access to Social Security benefits, access to private pensions and savings contributes greatly to differences in the well-being of the two groups of elderly. Those who earn the most during their working lives contribute the most to the Social Security system and get the most benefits in return. Although Social Security moderates to some degree the level of inequality in public benefits by offering greater rates of return (i.e., larger benefits per dollar contributed) to those who make low contributions, no such moderating mechanisms exist for private pensions. High income before old age translates directly into high income during old age. Women, less educated workers, and minorities often do not have jobs that offer a private pension program and do not have the extra income to save for retirement on their own. If public social insurance programs favor the advantaged, private pensions do so even more.

The advantaged groups also get benefits from the tax system. Tax deductions for old age most favor those with the highest income; those who pay little or no taxes receive little benefit. Similarly, the policy of untaxed profits on the sale of a home for people age 55 and over favors high-income groups; the more expensive the home, the larger the price gain, the more the tax cut. Finally, the higher the contributions paid to private pension programs, the greater the deferred taxes.

Means-tested benefits such as SSI should favor the disadvantaged elderly and therefore moderate the differences between older people in the two worlds. Yet means-tested programs for the elderly face the same problems as means-tested programs in general. First, means-tested programs, often under government pressure to cut costs, strictly enforce rules for eligibility. Elderly people who saved too much before old age—despite low income—cannot gain benefits. Recipients who have earnings from part-time work that raise their income above a certain level lose SSI benefits. Gifts from family members count against the income or asset limit and can also result in loss of benefits. Even moving in with adult children whose incomes exceed the limit results in loss of benefits. The bureaucratic rules required to prove low income and high need discourage many from applying for the benefits.

Second, even full SSI benefits do not alone provide for a decent living. Benefits leave recipients who are without other benefits below the poverty line. Income from other sources, including income from other types of means-tested programs, can push elderly people above the poverty line, but just barely. Although percentages below poverty have declined, many elderly people remain in near-poverty status.

Third, recipients of SSI lack the political power of the more advantaged elderly recipients of Social Security to battle for more generous benefits. The infirm, single, poor, female, and minority elderly lack organizations, advocates, and high levels of political activity. Despite their obvious need, these groups did not make the contributions to the system that others did, and they have a harder time making claims for more benefits. Like all means-tested programs, SSI receives limited funds: Only 2.7 percent of public expenditures for the elderly in 1990 went to SSI (U.S. Bureau of the Census 1994:371).

Another source of inequality in old age—and a special problem for public policies—involves dealing with serious problems of health, disability, and mental impairment. Although benefits help healthy retirees, they do less to alleviate problems of living produced by chronic disease. Those with disabilities find it difficult to drive, walk long distances, climb stairways, or shop. Without help, they often cannot cook, clean, move around their homes, or visit friends or relatives. Yet help for these crucial daily activities proves expensive if friends or family members cannot provide it. Public programs do not routinely cover these costs.

Other older people face health problems that require long periods of rehabilitation, special treatment, and immense medical costs. Heart disease, cancer, kidney failure, and strokes may require people to spend their life savings before receiving public benefits. Despite plans for a comfortable retirement, a catastrophic illness can leave older people destitute if they lack some other source of private insurance.

Problems of mental impairment that afflict a minority of elderly people, such as Alzheimer's disease and other forms of dementia, also create public policy problems of support. The treatment of Alzheimer's disease, for example, requires nearly continuous supervision that places intolerable burdens on caretakers. Family members have immense difficulties caring for loved ones with Alzheimer's disease. Furthermore, because hiring full-time private home care costs so much money, institutionalization becomes the only solution (Margolis 1990).

The usual Social Security and Medicare benefits do not deal well with these kinds of problems. Programs aimed toward the typical retiree do not provide for the extreme costs faced by those with severe health problems. In fact, those with the greatest health needs, who require the most assistance and have the highest costs, typically have the lowest incomes. Older, unmarried, and female elderly people typically qualify only for the minimum Social Security benefit, but most risk long-term disability and poor health. Eventually, these people may have to rely on means-tested programs.

In contrast, the more advantaged elderly can rely on private health care insurance benefits. Because Medicare on average covers only about 44 percent of health costs, the more affluent elderly purchase private insurance to cover what Medicare does not (Smeeding 1990:374). Such insurance can cover longer hospital stays, specialized procedures, expensive services, and minor problems. The poor who rely on public benefits alone do not get the same quality medical care.

These problems suggest that considerable diversity exists among the aged population (Quinn 1987). Although most old people enjoy affluence, leisure, and high levels of public support, many others nevertheless face poverty, poor health, and dependence. These inequalities result directly from the dual nature of old age policy. Critics emphasize the role of the government in producing inequality between the advantaged and disadvantaged elderly, and they highlight the failures rather than the successes of public policy.

The Politics of Inequality

Having begun in the previous chapter with two images of old age, one emphasizing vulnerability and one emphasizing advantage, and having ended with two views of old-age public policy, one emphasizing successes and one emphasizing failures, this chapter needs to connect image and policy. In simple terms, the view of vulnerability in old age emphasizes policy failures, whereas the view of the elderly as advantaged emphasizes policy successes. In more complex terms, however, political ideology colors viewpoints concerning the outcomes of public policy for the elderly. Competing political beliefs can recognize both success and failure but interpret quite differently the causes of success and the remedies needed to deal with the failures. These competing beliefs have special relevance to debates over public spending.

On one hand, by emphasizing the advantaged image of the elderly, more conservative political views question the value of some of the public spending on older people. Although expenditures for older people and Social Security represent a major portion of the federal budget, a large portion of the funds go to the already affluent members of the middle class whose private pensions and savings could support them quite nicely (if not luxuriously) in old age. At the same time the affluent receive generous retirement benefits, workers struggle to pay taxes and support their families. In this sense, old age policies do not efficiently distribute resources.

If such spending patterns did not in the past create problems, the growth of government deficits now means they contribute crucially to fiscal problems. The government has spent more than it takes in every year since 1973, and accumulated deficits represent astounding amounts—$234 billion in 1994 and $4.2 trillion in the past 20 years. Although by no means the cause of deficit spending, Social Security represents a major portion of the budget and a potential source of spending cuts in the eyes of many critics. Savings gained from reduced Social Security could go to debt payoff and to spending on other social problems.

A conservative remedy to the problems of inequality in old age and deficit spending advocates more careful targeting of benefits to those in most need. In the short run, changes in Social Security would reduce benefits for those elderly with relatively high private income. In the long run, changes to Social Security would encourage workers to rely more on private pensions, savings, and individual retirement accounts. Public programs would reserve benefits for those most in need. According to advocates, this would reduce inequality by concentrating public efforts on the most disadvantaged while allowing for the private sector to provide support for most retirees. It would also reduce overall levels of spending, free funds for other purposes, and reduce the taxes of younger workers. Such recommendations follow from more general suspicions of conservatives about the effectiveness and value of government programs.

On the other hand, more liberal political views, in emphasizing the vulnerable image of the elderly, suggest the state has not gone far enough in support of older people. Current policies help many in need, but not as many as they should. Advocates of this view favor universal programs like those in many European nations. Benefits would become widely available to the elderly, even without previous contributions, substantial earnings, or labor market success.

Liberal views oppose efforts to shift retirement support from government programs to private investments. Such efforts to privatize Social Security will link benefits more closely to market income. Despite their own concerns with the nature of existing programs, liberals see conservative criticisms of Social Security as an attempt to undermine altogether the government's role in providing social protection. They believe that reducing government involvement in the support of the elderly would promote inequality rather than reduce it. Governments should become more rather than less involved in old-age pensions.

A successful program should unify all segments of the population—young and old, advantaged and disadvantaged—in support of the program. Making Social Security private would instead increase the distinction between those depending on generous private benefits and those depending on means-tested public programs. In the liberal view, fewer distinctions in benefits would provide the most effective means to reduce inequality, and policy changes should expand benefits for everyone equally.

Debates between conservatives and liberals in Congress and the business community now dominate discussion of Social Security. Those opposed to changes in Social Security, like Senator Moynihan, worry about the criticisms of a successful program.

> *"DANIEL PATRICK MOYNIHAN can be a gloomy Irishman, but over the years Washington has learned to listen to [him]. . . . The senior senator from New York, who advised both John F. Kennedy and Richard Nixon, has been trying to shore up the welfare state since he was a professor at Harvard in the 1960s. Lately, he has heard the foundations cracking. Last week Moynihan sat in his darkened office on Capitol Hill, unhappily contemplating the uncertain future of Social Security. He noted that most Americans have given up on the program. . . . They have lost faith in perhaps the most successful federal program ever. . . . If Social Security 'goes private,' Moynihan says, 'you're going to lose it. It won't be there.' Poor people who don't have bank accounts, much less stockbrokers, would be left in what would become essentially a welfare program. Everyone else would take his chances in the market—and if the market crashed, as it well could, they would be out of luck."*
> *(Thomas 1997:21)*

Others see much room for improvement in the current system. In 1997, the Advisory Council on Social Security recommended investment of Security contributions in the stock market.

> *THOMAS JONES, decades younger than Moynihan, has devoted his career to business and the private sector rather than to the government and public*

service. He has a completely different viewpoint on Social Security than Moynihan. Jones is president of TIAA-CREF, a company that invests the private pension contributions of employees of universities and non-profit organizations. Those belongings to TIAA-CREF have seen their contributions grow tremendously under Jones' investments in stocks and bonds. Then why not invest Social Security benefits as well, and allow current workers to get the benefits of growth in the stock market when they retire? To Jones, it makes more economic sense to invest contributions to Social Security than immediately spend them or let other parts of the government borrow them. By following the lead of successful private pension companies, the government could increase future benefits for many without increasing taxes now. To younger people who never expect to see benefits under the current system, such a prospect has some appeal (Sloan 1997:28).

Given the diversity of experiences in old age, policy changes in the future will likely fall somewhere between the goals of universality and program expansion and the goals of privatization and high economic returns. Still, these viewpoints frame current political debates.

Conclusion

Care of older adults was once a private matter, yet the government has become crucial in providing economic support for the elderly in modern societies. In addition, government policies have come to help define the nature and boundaries of aging. Because many older people could not survive without Social Security benefits, and many others rely on Social Security to make life better, the study of aging and social policy is inseparable.

Public support for the elderly has resulted in both successes and failures. The successes are evident in impressive drops in poverty and rising income. The average elderly person in the 1990s has more income, a more comfortable lifestyle, and a greater sense of pride and satisfaction than in past decades. These improvements stem in large part from public policy. The success of policies for the elderly relate to the social insurance nature of programs that link workers and retirees in a type of generational agreement. No other programs for younger age groups have gained the public support or enjoy the same generosity of benefits as Social Security or Medicare.

At the same time, Social Security and Medicare by their very nature deal less well with a minority of the elderly. These people have contributed little to the Social Security system, have little in the way of private pensions and savings, and may experience severe health problems. Older people in these circumstances depend on poorly funded and less popular means-tested programs rather than on social insurance programs. The differences in support generate inequality in old age and create risks of financial deprivation for many.

The dual nature of old age—both the triumph and tragedy—emphasizes the importance of inequality in old age and the role of social policy in producing this inequality. The status of the elderly reflects considerable diversity in the United States. Other high-income nations also show inequality in old age, but they provide universal public pension benefits that moderate this inequality more than in the United States. Beyond these general statements, however, little agreement exists on the proper solutions to the problems of old age. Among policymakers, conservative advocates of reliance on private pensions compete with liberal advocates of expanded public benefits. In these times of deficit spending, conservatives have considerable influence in Washington, but the widespread support for Social Security among the young and old has counterbalanced such influence.

3

Class Differences before and during Old Age

HELEN AND HER HUSBAND lived modestly during most of her adult life. Located in a small town of about 1500 people in the rural Midwest, Helen taught elementary school and her husband was part owner of a small business. Because both had college degrees, they had better opportunities than most others in their community. Still, having grown up during the Depression, they worried about finances, spent carefully, and saved as much as they could. In their household, showers over a few minutes were not allowed because they wasted water, long-distance phone calls were too expensive except on holidays, aluminum foil and plastic bags were washed and reused, and the children had little in the way of spending money. Of course, small-town living offered few temptations to purchase luxuries. Housing was inexpensive, entertainment consisted mostly of socializing with relatives and neighbors, and commuting involved walking to nearby work and school. After putting the children through state colleges, Helen's husband sold the business and retired. Unfortunately, he died not long afterward. To her surprise, Helen discovered that with life insurance, savings, Social Security benefits, and a house with no mortgage, she was quite well off. After decades of saving, Helen entered old age with a sense of financial security that she had never felt before. She could retire, rely on Social Security benefits for daily living expenses, and use her savings for travel, a new car, a nicer house, and medical and nursing home insurance. To be honest, she never had it so good.

EDWARD HAD JUST THE OPPOSITE EXPERIENCE: After doing well economically during his work life, he found himself quite poor during old age. He grew up in a working-class neighborhood in Chicago. His father worked in the trucking industry, and his mother was a homemaker. Compared to others in the neighborhood, Edward and his family did pretty well during the Depression because his father always had work. After fighting in Europe during World War II, Edward returned to Chicago, finished two

years of college, and got married. Working as a salesman, he lived on com-
missions and often had to struggle financially during the next 20 to 30 years.
Still, times were pretty good during the 1950s and 1960s, and Edward
viewed his life as challenging but "a pretty good deal." As he approached old
age, however, things took a turn for the worse. He and his wife divorced, and
he began to have problems with his legs. Eventually, he had to have both legs
amputated because of a bone disease, and he was moved to a nursing home.
He disliked living in the nursing home so much that he moved to a cheap,
run-down hotel. At the hotel, he made friends who offered companionship
and assistance in buying groceries. Yet with only a few thousand dollars in
Social Security benefits and confined to a wheelchair, Edward found life more
difficult than ever. Although never well off, he felt more deprived now than
during middle age (Rollinson 1990).

These two stories illustrate an important point about the economic
status of elderly people. People evaluate their experiences in old age relative to their experiences in earlier adulthood. Whereas Helen feels especially well off because she has more money to spend than in the past,
Edward experiences his deprivation more intensely because he has much
less. Although many experience circumstances in old age quite similar to
those before old age, the potential exists for substantial changes to occur
in late life.

The possibility for changes in late life suggests the need to compare
social and economic status of people before and during old age. The previous chapters identified two worlds of aging that define quite different
experiences and characteristics of older people. Although the existence of
the two worlds implies a fair degree of inequality, it says little about the
relationship of this inequality to inequality before old age. After all, social
and economic differences also exist in middle age. The question then becomes: How do these differences before old age compare to those during
old age?

This question highlights the connection between age and social class.
Social classes consist of groups of people who share similar social resources such as income, prestige, and power. Class inequality exists before old age, and, as demonstrated in Chapter 1, social class represents a
crucial source of differences in the experiences of old age. Yet class inequality may combine with inequality across age groups to define quite
different experiences between people who enter old age with many resources and those who enter old age with fewer resources.

This question also relates to debates over the influence of public policies on the lives of the elderly. Retirement involves striking changes in

public and private sources of income. Before old age and retirement, economic status depends in large part on the private labor market and wage and salary income. After retirement, economic status depends more on public pension benefits. If government benefits are distributed more equally than wage and salary income, then class differences should emerge smaller during old age than earlier. If not, the opposite should occur.

This chapter examines how old age and public policies for the elderly affect class differences (and, conversely, how class differences affect experiences in old age). The next section considers how class and age combine to affect social and economic well-being. On one hand, the equalizing effects of government programs tend to reduce class differences from middle age to old age. On the other hand, private pensions and savings tend to increase or maintain class inequality from middle age to old age. Although simplified, these two perspectives offer a useful way to begin the discussion. The remainder of the chapter reviews the evidence, identifying circumstances that both promote and moderate class differences in old age and thereby contribute to diversity.

Stability and Change in Inequality from Middle Age to Old Age

To help clarify the nature of class differences among the elderly, I begin with a review of sources of both equality and inequality in old age. As in the previous chapter, the arguments in this chapter correspond roughly to more general arguments about policy successes and failures. However, they specifically address the issue of inequality from the perspective of life course changes from middle to old age.

Sources of Declining Inequality in Old Age

In some ways, old age and retirement benefits reduce inequality and the size of the class differences that exist before old age. In concrete terms, this type of change shows in the contrast between the economic resources of a lawyer, doctor, or corporate executive with those of a cab driver, construction worker, or factory employee. Professionals have substantially higher income than do blue-collar workers during their work lives and can accumulate considerably more assets such as homes, investments, cars, furniture, and private pensions. Does the gap in social and economic resources between these two groups of workers change in old age? In some ways, it does—the gap may become smaller because of retirees' increased reliance on public programs. It is not that, as a group, professionals end up no better off than workers during old age or that class differences disappear; rather, economic resources on average become more similar after retirement.

> TAKE, FOR EXAMPLE, *the experiences of two brothers, Frank and Vincent. Frank liked school more than Vincent, went to college to study accounting, and joined a firm downtown in a large city. Vincent did not care all that much for studying and joined a construction firm as a carpenter after high school. Over the years, the financial circumstances of Frank improved compared with those of Vincent. Frank had substantially higher income and could afford a nicer home, better furnishings, a more expensive car, and private schools for his kids. During the next 30 or 40 years, Vincent did fine but felt poor relative to his more successful brother. However, when they both retired, the differences in their lifestyles diminished. Frank received more Social Security and private pension income than did Vincent, but the differences were much smaller than their differences in salary. Vincent could not afford an expensive lifestyle, but, without the high salary of his job, neither could Frank. The brothers found they had much more in common during old age and retirement than they did as adults in the labor force.*

Multiplied across millions of people, this pattern would suggest smaller class differences in old age than in earlier adulthood.

According to the argument, greater equality in old age results from the more equal distribution of government benefits compared to private sector wages, salaries, investments, and self-employed income. Throughout the history of the Social Security system, low-income workers have received a greater rate of return on their contributions to Social Security than have high-income workers. A few details on how the program determines benefit levels illustrate the varying rates of return. The formula to determine benefits aims to replace a certain portion of the worker's previous earnings, but it replaces a larger portion of earnings for low-income workers than for high-income workers. For example, a worker retiring in 1992 at age 65 with 1991 earnings of $20,000 gets $13,464 per year in benefits (Rejda 1994:111). A worker with earnings of $50,000 gets $19,452 per year in benefits. The lower-income worker gets benefits equal to 67 percent of previous earnings, whereas the higher-income worker gets benefits equal to 39 percent of previous earnings. Because they contributed more, higher-income workers get more benefits—$19,452 versus

$13,464. However, low-income workers receive a higher *percentage* of their earnings in Social Security benefits. Because of this formula, the gap in benefits between high- and low-income workers declines compared to the gap in earnings: The earnings differ by $30,000, whereas the benefits differ by $5,988.

The extent to which Social Security favors low-income workers shows in Figure 3.1. The first two bars display the advantage in earnings (in thousands of dollars) of a high-income worker relative to a low-income worker. The next two bars suggest a much smaller advantage (again in thousands of dollars) of the high-income workers in Social Security benefits. Finally, the last two bars reveal the percentage of earnings replaced by Social Security. This replacement percentage is actually higher for low-income workers than for high-income workers.

Medicare benefits may also favor the disadvantaged more than the well off. Medicare offers benefits to all Social Security recipients on the basis of health care needs rather than on earlier contributions. Unlike for normal retirement benefits, those contributing the most to Social Security do not qualify for more health care benefits. Furthermore, if people with low income during adulthood experience more health problems in old age, they will use the available health care benefits more than higher-income people. With equal access of all people to health care during old age, lower-class people, by virtue of worse health, may actually get more Medicare benefits than others. Although not in the form of cash, such benefits can still reduce inequality.

The availability of need-based benefits for the poor, such as Supplemental Security Income (SSI), obviously favors those with low income. Although benefits for SSI fall well below normal Social Security benefits, they go directly to those most in need. Older people with no other income receive a guaranteed monthly check from SSI if they do not own assets (excluding home, auto, and some household goods) worth more than $2000 for an individual or $3000 for a couple (Rejda 1994:421). Other means-tested programs such as food stamps, public housing, and Medicaid also offer benefits only to low-income elderly.

These components of public programs for older people tend to favor those with less education, lower-status jobs, and lower market income relative to those with more advantages during middle age. The programs tend to reduce the gap in income in old age compared to the gap that exists at preretirement ages. Income of all groups may fall from middle to old age, but it falls more for high-income groups than for low-income groups.

FIGURE 3.1

Social Security Replacement of Earnings

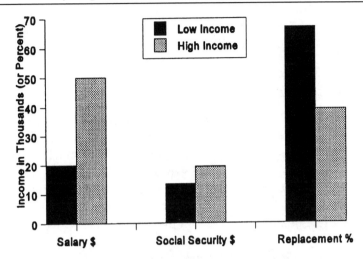

Public policies in the United States could, like policies in many European nations, do more to reduce inequality (Huber, Ragin, and Stephens 1993). Still, the essential point is that expansion of public support in old age in recent decades has most improved the lives of the worst off. Social Security does not do all that much to support the well off—they do fine on their own—but it helps the disadvantaged.

Why do public programs help reduce inequality in old age? Because democratic governments count votes equally among citizens, those groups with fewer resources and power but larger numbers can still influence the political process. Unlike the private labor market, the government responds to the needs of all voters with equalizing policies in old age, thus potentially reducing status differences.

A useful way to present the implications of these arguments comes from graphing the expected changes in income during old age. Assume that, averaged over all people, income levels decline as people reach old age for the simple reason that workers obtain more income than retirees. The average relationship between age and income would produce a downward sloping line as in Figure 3.2. However, by considering changes in income separately for high- and low-status groups, arguments for declining inequality make a more precise prediction: Income would drop most for the high-status group because its members have the most to lose in shifting from private income sources to public sources.

The low-status group, given the equalizing impact of public programs, would experience a smaller decline. Figure 3.2, by graphing the different patterns for high- and low-status groups, reveals changes in the spread around the average. The gap between the income of the high- and low-status groups falls from middle age to old age.

Sources of Increasing Inequality in Old Age

Other sources of income in old age may actually increase previous differences in social positions. Economic resources of high-status workers before retirement contribute to relatively high private pension benefits, savings, and assets after retirement. Even if sources and levels of income change, middle- and upper-class groups still enjoy special advantages in old age.

To illustrate potential increases in inequality, consider again the contrast in economic resources between professionals and blue-collar workers. Not only do professionals earn more, they can use their higher earnings for pensions and savings to help support themselves in old age. Even if blue-collar retirees receive public pensions similar to those of professionals, they will have less private income during old age.

TAKE THE EXPERIENCE OF TWO SISTERS, Rebecca and Jennifer. Both attended the same college and became schoolteachers. They lived similar lives near the suburban schools they taught at, both marrying, having two children, and continuing to work until near retirement. However, Rebecca taught at a public high school with a generous salary and pension plan. She could also afford to invest part of her salary in stocks and bonds for retirement. In contrast, Jennifer taught at a lower-paying, private day care center without a pension plan. She had little extra money to save for retirement. Besides the differences in savings and private pensions, the daily living expenses of the two sisters were much the same. Both Jennifer and Rebecca could rely on their earnings to help support their family. Upon retirement, however, their economic experiences began to diverge. Jennifer began to experience serious health problems. Medicare covered most of the costs, but, lacking a private pension and savings, she had little left to pay for normal living expenses. In contrast, Rebecca could supplement her Social Security benefits with private pension benefits and income from investments and savings. She could continue spending much as she had before retirement and barely noticed a change in her economic well-being. However similar their lives as adults, Rebecca and Jennifer experienced strikingly different lives as retirees.

FIGURE 3.2

Predictions of Declining Inequality

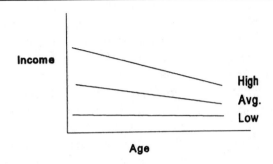

Why would old age increase class differences? Most would agree that old age involves stressful changes in work, family, and health that threaten the financial well-being of individuals and couples. If so, the more savings, investments, private pensions, home equity, and other assets people accumulate during their work years, the more resources they have to help them deal with the financial problems of old age (Dannefer 1987; O'Rand 1996). Elderly individuals lacking such resources find themselves especially vulnerable to income problems (Ross and Wu 1996). The unequal distribution of private resources in earlier adulthood thus contributes to class differences in old age, and public transfers cannot make up for the differences.

More specifically, middle- and upper-class groups bring several advantages into old age that maintain or increase their relative economic position. First, earnings remain an important, although not dominant, source of income in old age. As shown earlier, 18 percent of the income of people over age 65 in 1990 came from earnings (Moon and Ruggles 1994). These earnings likely contribute to inequality in old age as they do earlier. Second, private pensions often provide benefits based directly on previous earnings. Because inequality in earnings exists, so does inequality in private pension benefits. Also, because some workers do not qualify for any private pension programs, the gap in private pensions may be greater than the gap in wages. Third, those with higher incomes during adulthood have more assets, such as savings, expensive homes and possessions, and investments that provide actual income or comfort during old age. Savings and investments account for a surprisingly large part of the income of the elderly—25 percent in 1990 (Moon and Ruggles 1994).

With higher income in old age, middle- and upper-class groups can afford better health insurance and medical care. The Medicare program provides insurance for hospital care and physician's fees, but these benefits cover less than half of all medical costs of the elderly (Smeeding 1990:374). Medicaid covers medical costs for those elderly with extremely low income but aids only a small part of the aged population. Private companies offer "medigap" insurance to pay benefits for medical services uncovered by the public programs. Those able to purchase this type of private insurance may get better medical care than those who, for financial reasons, must depend completely on Medicare or Medicaid.

The continued importance of private income in old age thus strengthens the position of those with high education, high-status jobs, and high market income during middle age relative to those with fewer advantages. Differences in private income also counter the influence of public programs and keep class differences as large in old age as in middle age. Therefore, the gap in income in old age compared to the gap in preretirement ages increases.

The continued importance of private income in old age also means that the government does little to reduce the influence of the private market in capitalist societies. When intended as a supplement to private income, government policies for older people maintain the advantages of more powerful groups. Interest groups for older people that exert strong influence on public policy may, for example, favor the interests of relatively advantaged segments of the elderly (Estes 1993; Minkler 1991). As a result, Social Security historically has avoided payment rules that would drastically reorder class rankings in society (Cates 1983).

Another version of this argument also denies that public programs reduce inequality, and it suggests that, on average, aging maintains previous class differences. In other words, the forces producing diversity counteract the forces producing similarity. Although examples of both declining inequality and increasing inequality exist, the more typical pattern would involve *maintenance* of class differences. Because public income sources promote greater equality and private income sources promote greater inequality, all sources together keep differences pretty much the same from middle age to old age.

To illustrate the effect of private income sources on inequality in old age, Figure 3.3a graphs changes in income for low- and high-status groups as they grow old. In contrast to Figure 3.2, this graph implies that the income of low-status groups falls more than high-status groups. Consequently, the income gap grows at the older ages. Figure 3.3b illustrates maintenance of class differences by showing parallel lines for high- and

FIGURE 3.3

Predictions of Continuing or Increasing Inequality

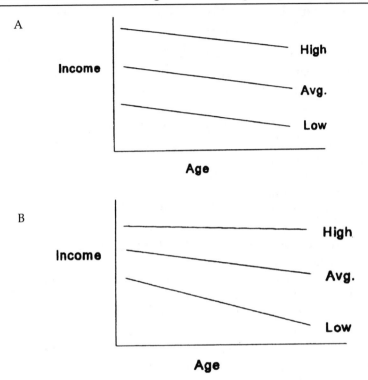

low-income groups. Consistent with continuing inequality, income declines as people grow older at the same rate for low-income and high-income people.

Studying Changes over the Life Course

Researchers have used several types of methods to study aging:

- *Cross-sectional* methods examine age groups at one single point in time. Comparisons of middle-aged people with elderly people may reveal important differences.

- *Time-series* methods focus on trends or changes over time in the aged population that compare elderly people in different historical periods.

- ■   *Longitudinal* methods follow the same group of people as they grow old. Observing the same people at several different ages allows researchers to understand how individuals change as they enter different life stages.

For the purpose of testing arguments about changes in inequality before and after old age, longitudinal methods are superior. Cross-sectional data, such as those provided by government surveys and census figures, can usefully describe differences in work, health, and income levels across groups of nonelderly and elderly people. Rather than presenting a motion picture of the life of the same people from middle age to old age, however, cross-sectional data provide a snapshot of different age groups or generations. Cross-sectional figures cannot capture what occurs before or after that particular picture.

Consider your own family. You differ from your parents and grandparents in part because you are younger. However, given social change and generational experiences, you will no doubt differ in important ways from your parents when you reach middle age and from your grandparents when you reach old age. Cross-sectional comparisons can imply incorrectly that aging will be the same for you as it was for your parents and grandparents. A one-time comparison will fail to reveal how aging differs across generations.

Time-series methods focusing on yearly changes in characteristics of the elderly also have limitations. Trends over time show rising retirement, higher life expectancy, greater reliance on public pension income, and reductions in poverty. Much the way your grandparents currently differ from your great-grandparents, today's elderly differ from the elderly 25 years ago.

To study trends over time, researchers must compare different groups of elderly or distinct generations. For the most part, the elderly population in the 1950s does not contain the same people as in the 1990s. Furthermore, each generation brings different experiences and backgrounds into old age. For example, many elderly people who had below-poverty income in the 1950s may also have faced similar circumstances as adults during the Great Depression of the 1930s. Relative to their adult years, their elderly years in the 1950s may not have seemed substantially worse. In contrast, elderly people with income barely above poverty levels in the 1990s may well have enjoyed substantially higher income during their adult years. Despite low levels of poverty, the current elderly may feel deprived relative to their previous income. Given the different backgrounds of older people in the 1950s and the 1990s, trends among the elderly may be misleading.

The study of aging thus creates problems for research studies. Neither cross-sectional nor trend data adequately capture the changes that occur to individuals during the process of aging. Although an expensive and difficult alternative, longitudinal data have become increasingly important in research studies. Relying primarily on longitudinal studies, the next sections review the evidence on class-based change and stability in work, health, poverty, and income from middle age to old age.

Changes in Work and Retirement

Cross-sectional data show what most of us know already. Fewer people work during old age than during middle age. In 1993, 16 percent of men and 8 percent of women age 65 and over participated in the labor force (including full-time workers, part-time workers, and unemployed people actively looking for work). For men ages 45 to 54 and 55 to 64, 90 percent and 66 percent, respectively, participated in the labor force; for women at the same ages, 74 percent and 47 percent, respectively, participated (U.S. Bureau of the Census 1994:395). Such figures match our commonsense definition of retirement as withdrawal from the paid labor force during old age.

Perhaps just as obviously, time-series data show that the number of retirees has increased in recent decades. Compared to the 16 percent figure in 1993, 27 percent of men age 65 and over worked in 1970. Not only do more older people retire now than in the past, but the age of retirement has fallen in recent decades as well (Gendell and Siegel 1996). As a result of early retirement, the labor force participation rate of men ages 55 to 64 fell from 83 percent in 1970 to 66 percent in 1993. Compared to earlier generations, recent generations reaching old age have more and younger retirees.

Despite clear differences across age groups and time periods in work and retirement, longitudinal data reveal complexity not shown by other types of data. Following workers as they grow older discloses a gradual retirement process for most people (Ruhm 1990). Stereotypes often distinguish middle-aged people who work full-time and live on wage and salary income from retired people who do not work for pay and live on private and public old-age pension benefits. The two extremes clearly differ, but the stages leading from one to the other appear less precise (Mutchler et al. 1997).

Although many experience an abrupt shift from work status to retirement status, many others hold "bridge" jobs between full-time work and complete retirement (Doeringer 1990). Some workers retire partially, working part-time before withdrawing from the labor force altogether. Others retire from one job, then begin another while receiving a pension from the first. Some retire but then reenter the labor force after finding retirement too boring or their income too low. Some would like to keep working but retire after they lose their jobs and are unable to find another. Some may leave the labor force early for reasons of disability rather than retirement, but for practical purposes, they appear retired. Still others keep working until death or serious illness.

Although estimates vary, a recent study suggests that 33 percent of retirees eventually reenter the labor force (Hayward, Hardy, and Liu 1994). Most of them quickly realized that, for any number of reasons, they found retirement unsatisfactory. They typically reenter within two years, mostly in full-time rather than part-time employment. Given the high likelihood of returning to the labor force for one-third of retirees, the transition from work to retirement becomes an ambiguous event—permanent for most, but temporary for many others.

Many people reaching old age want to continue working. Consider 79-year-old Mike Wallace, correspondent for *60 Minutes*; 94-year-old Strom Thurmond, senator from South Carolina; and 88-year old Jessica Tandy, star of the Academy Award-winning movie *Driving Miss Daisy*. Christensen (1990) describes several less well-known examples of work during old age:

> *JOE DOES NOT NEED TO WORK. At 65 years old, he receives Social Security and private pension benefits, his wife still works, and they own their home outright. Still, after 40 years as a police officer, it took only one month of boredom at home as a retiree to convince him that he still wanted to work. When he found a local bank willing to hire him as a security guard for three nights a week, he jumped at the chance. Christensen notes that "He works cheaper than most guards because he is paid off the books and, in addition, he knew that he could make extra money through kickbacks from delivery boys and repairmen." Along with the additional activity, he welcomes the extra tax-free $5000 a year (Christensen 1990:184-86).*

> *MICHAEL MAKES EXTRA MONEY working for himself. Also 65 years old, he retired from work for the federal government because of a bad back and*

heart problems. Needing less vigorous work, he began to deliver cars for dealers in the New York City area. The work pays fairly well but is irregular. Fortunately, he can rely on a civil service pension and use the extra money he gets as it comes along. Despite the burden of filling out forms that all self-employed people face, he likes the job and "intends to keep working because of financial need and the desire to keep active. . . . Working provides self-esteem and a clear sense of identity (Christensen 1990:191-2).

In many other cases, however, working during old age or returning to work after retirement reflects economic need. Neither person described below by Calasanti and Bonanno (1992:143-44) can remain fully retired.

DORIS RETIRED FROM A LARGE COMPANY during a time of slow production and employee layoffs. She can get by on Social Security, but not easily. Any extra money helps with daily living expenses. The authors state that "Over the last several years, she has worked as a temporary who cleans files for the state and as a 'private duty nurse,' a minimum-wage role that required two days of training" (p. 143). She also works as a temporary for the same company she worked for before retirement (ironically at a higher wage). Marie retired in her late 50s because of poor health. Having worked at low pay for the past 20 years, she found that her job offered a pension of less than $100 a month. Not nearly enough to support her living expenses, Marie sews things at home to sell. Her products sell for little, especially compared to the time she has to put in on them, but they help pay for medicine. She simply could not survive without working during her retirement.

The complexity of retirement makes it difficult to employ a simple definition. Parnes and Less (1985), for example, create three indicators of retirement in their study: (a) self-identification as retired, (b) not working in the paid labor force, and (c) receipt of a pension. They find that by ages 60 to 74, 86 percent of the sample meet at least one of the conditions, but only 41 percent meet all three. Most retirees fall somewhere between the extremes of satisfying all conditions and satisfying none of the conditions.

Elder and Pavalko (1993) provide another classification of retirement types. They identify 30 percent of their sample as having retired abruptly and 8 percent as having not retired at all. The other 62 percent retired gradually or moved back and forth from work and retirement. In addition, they found that members of more recent elderly generations show more gradual and sporadic retirement than do older elderly generations. As retirement has become more common, the transition has become more complex.

Despite difficulties in definition and measurement, nearly all studies demonstrate class differences in retirement. In short, the higher the social class or status of workers, the longer they work. Furthermore, the higher the social class or status of retirees, the more likely that they will reenter the labor force. These differences in the likelihood of retirement have important consequences for class differences in income during old age.

More specifically, the occupation held longest during a person's working career relates most closely to retirement. If a person changes jobs for a short period before retirement, the most recently held job will not accurately predict retirement behavior. Based on the occupational category of the longest job, studies find that higher-status, white-collar workers—professionals, managers, sales workers—are least likely to retire (Hayward and Grady 1990). Lower-status clerical and blue-collar workers—skilled laborers, unskilled laborers, and machine and vehicle operators—are most likely to retire.

Workers with higher-prestige jobs likely have more opportunities to continue working. Professional, managerial, and sales workers perform less physically demanding tasks than do blue-collar workers, and physical demands of a job increase the likelihood of injury, disability, and early retirement (Hayward et al. 1989). In addition, the more flexible work schedules of professional and sales jobs allow part-time work without complete retirement. The benefits of flexibility for continued work also appear in the low rates of retirement of self-employed workers, who can adjust their work hours and schedules to suit their needs and interests in old age.

Workers with higher-prestige jobs also have greater incentives to continue working. They enjoy work more and gain more financially. For example, Hayward et al. (1989) find that workers in jobs that involve complex tasks have lower rates of retirement, perhaps because the challenge keeps workers interested in their jobs. The higher salary of high-prestige workers also makes retirement less attractive.

Consistent with these occupational differences, more highly educated workers are less likely to retire (Palmore et al. 1985). Compared to others, college-educated people have higher-status occupations, which would reduce retirement. In addition, college-educated people enjoy more challenging work, earn higher wages, face less physically demanding tasks, and have skills in high demand by employers. All of these factors contribute to lower retirement.

Along with having lower rates of retirement, high-status and highly educated workers are more likely to reenter the labor force after retirement (Hayward and Grady 1990). Because higher-status workers tend to have better pension coverage and higher private benefits (Clark, Ghent, and Headen 1994), it makes sense that many will retire from one job to receive a private pension, then enter into another job to supplement their income. Many lower-status people reenter the labor force because of economic need, but they do not have the same opportunity to find another job as do higher-status workers.

The differences in retirement rates between high-prestige, better educated workers and low-prestige, less educated workers do not mean that retirement is forced on those with low status—quite the contrary. People from all status backgrounds want to retire. As Crowley (1985) states, "All in all, retirement does not seem to produce any negative effects on well-being, at least in the initial years. If anything, men find that retirement is better than they thought it would be" (p. 169). When problems do occur during retirement, they come not from lack of work but from poor health or low income.

However, should they desire not to retire, high-status people will have more opportunities to realize their desires. As a result, high-status people approaching retirement age can better maintain their standard of living, keep active with challenging work, and mix work with leisure. If they do shift jobs during old age or find themselves unemployed late in life, those with high education and experience in high-prestige occupations can obtain better paying and more satisfying jobs than others. However complex and ambiguous retirement has become in modern societies, higher social class gives advantages during this process of change in labor force activity. Rather than disappearing as a source of inequality after exit from the labor force, class differences influence who retires, their retirement age, and their reasons for retirement.

Changes in Health, Disability, and Mortality

Cross-sectional data reveal poorer health, greater disability, and higher death rates among people over age 65 compared to those under age 65. Furthermore, people age 75 and over face higher risks of health problems, disability, and death than do people ages 65 to 74. Most older people remain in good health, and serious problems affect only a minority. Still, compared to younger age groups, health risks increase in old age.

Time-series data demonstrate declining mortality and higher life expectancy in recent decades, but they give mixed evidence on health and disability. According to some, healthier lifestyles and improved medical procedures have reduced the prevalence of both disability and death among the elderly in the past decade (Manton et al. 1995). Others claim that longer life expectancy increases or keeps constant the prevalence of disability (Crimmins, Saito, and Reynolds 1997). Even if it results in periods of poor health for those at the oldest ages, however, the declining death rate among the elderly is viewed by nearly everyone as a positive development.

Although longitudinal data describe changes in health during old age similar to those described by cross-sectional and time-series data, they also identify more precisely how differences in social class affect changes in health. Healthy people obviously experience a more satisfying old age than those in poor health, and it turns out that those from higher class backgrounds enjoy better health. In one longitudinal study, Hayward and Grady (1990) follow men ages 45 to 59 in 1966 for the next 15 years. They find that professionals and managers are less likely to become disabled than those in clerical, service, and craft occupations. For men in the early years of old age, it makes sense that those in more physically demanding jobs would face injury more often. Another longitudinal study shows that education also reduces disability among older people (Rogers, Rogers, and Berlanger 1992).

Similar findings come from a study of even older men and women in Sweden (Parker, Thorslund, and Lundberg 1994). To see if social class differences in disability remain well after retirement, the study examines people ages 77 to 98. It measures disability in terms of limitations in (a) daily activities such as bathing, dressing, cooking, and driving; (b) mobility or movement such as walking and climbing stairs; and (c) strength and body motion. It further compares these limitations or disabilities for four social classes defined by the occupation held longest during working life: white collar, skilled blue collar, unskilled blue collar, and self-employed (including farmers).

Figure 3.4 graphs the figures in Parker et al. (1994) and shows that occupation exerts a strong influence on disability, even among older people who typically had retired from the labor force many years ago. Among those with previous white-collar jobs, an average of 32 percent face limitations based on the three types of activities. Among those with previous unskilled blue-collar jobs, activity limitations reach an average of 51 percent. Compared to former white-collar workers, 19 percent more lower-status, former unskilled blue-collar workers face disability. Skilled blue-collar workers also have high rates of disability relative to white-collar workers.

FIGURE 3.4

Disability by Occupational Group

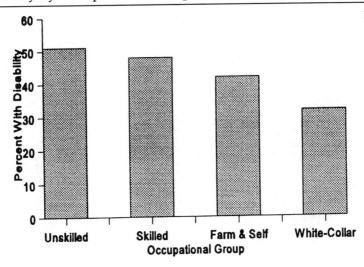

The same class differences that appear in disability during old age also appear in mortality. Studies dating back to the 1960s (Kitagawa and Hauser 1973) demonstrate that high education, income, and prestige reduce death rates (see Duleep [1989] for more recent data). Because these studies examine people of all ages, they attribute some of the mortality differences to exposure of low-status people to physically difficult or unsafe working conditions. However, because these researchers also find similar class differences in the mortality rates of spouses of high- and low-status workers, they also suggest that lifestyle and health care differences across classes affect mortality.

High levels of education, high occupational status, and high family income also have been found to lower mortality among men in their 50s and 60s (Moore 1990). Retired professionals live longer than people retired from lower-status jobs (Hayward and Grady 1990). Those with higher wealth experience lower death rates in old age, and those who lived in poverty before old age experience higher death rates in old age (Menchick 1993; see Wolfson et al. [1993] for similar results from a sample of older Canadian men). In terms of education, the mortality advantages of highly educated people have actually increased in recent years (Kunst and Mackenbach 1994). These class differences in mortality in old age may relate to class differences in smoking, alcohol, and other high-risk behaviors.

FIGURE 3.5

Survival by Status

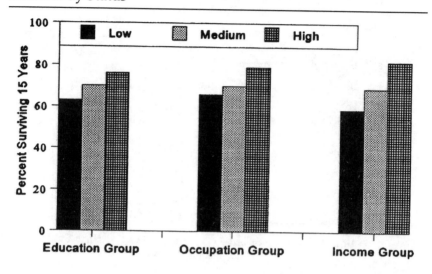

In reporting figures on class differences in mortality, Mott and Haurin (1985) nicely illustrate the consequences of social inequality. Using the same data analyzed in many other studies, Mott and Haurin examine the mortality rate of men ages 45 to 59 in 1966 over the next 15 years. They find that 76 percent of people with a high school degree survived compared to 63 percent of those with only a grade school education (see Figure 3.5). Applied to the millions of people approaching old age, the educational difference in survival of 13 percentage points translates into hundreds of thousands of early deaths for less educated people. Similarly, 79 percent of people with high-status jobs survived compared to 66 percent of people with low-status jobs. And 82 percent of people with high income survived compared to 60 percent of people with low income.

Making these comparisons over time reveals something else to indicate the importance of social class. Mortality has declined over the 15 years of Mott and Haurin's study, but it appears to have declined equally among all classes. As a result, the social class differences in mortality remained stable over time and continue to create diverse experiences in old age. Those from higher status or class backgrounds experience less disability and live longer than do those from lower status or class backgrounds, and they can enjoy a longer and more satisfying old age.

TABLE 3.1

Percentage below Poverty by Age Group in 1982 and 1992

1982		1992	
Age Group	% Poverty	Age Group	% Poverty
0-16	22.4	0-17	21.0
17-21	17.0	18-24	18.0
22-44	12.3	25-44	11.8
45-64	10.0	45-64	9.1
65+	16.0	65+	12.9

Changes in Poverty and Income

Poverty tarnishes the quality of life during old age, just as it does at younger ages. However, the seriousness of the problem of poverty during old age depends on the comparisons one makes and the type of data one uses. To illustrate these differences, Table 3.1 presents the percentage below poverty by age group in 1982 and 1992 (the two years employ somewhat different age groups).

On one hand, changes over time reveal improvements. The poverty rate among people over age 65 fell from 16.0 to 12.9 percent—a larger drop than that experienced by younger age groups. Other figures just for the elderly from 1959 and 1992 indicate an even larger change—from 35 percent below the poverty line to 13 percent (see Figure 1.1 in Chapter 1). As discussed earlier, the trends in public spending for each age group appear to match the trends in poverty. Public social insurance spending for the elderly in the form of Social Security benefits, Medicare, and disability rose dramatically in the past several decades. Many other factors affect poverty rates besides public spending, but spending is one important component. By reducing poverty, the upward trend in public spending seems to also reduce class differences during old age.

On the other hand, differences seen between age groups in Table 3.1 suggest some worsening of poverty during old age. In 1992, poverty is highest for people under age 21 and lowest for people 22 to 64, then increases from middle to old age. Longitudinal comparisons reveal the same life course pattern of poverty. Because many of the people ages 45 to 64 in 1982 had passed age 65 in 1992, a comparison of these two groups shows longitudinal changes. The poverty rate rises from 10 percent to 13 percent in making this comparison.

These age differences in poverty reflect the risks of sizable income loss as people enter old age. In a longitudinal study of people ages 66 to 74, Burkhauser and Duncan (1988) find that a substantial minority of 27 percent experienced a large drop of income (defined as income only half the size of previous income). Death of a spouse, a special problem for women, contributes to declining income; retirement often has the same consequence. Both events occur most commonly in old age, contributing to poverty. These findings present a less positive view of changes in income during old age than do time-series comparisons of different older generations.

The same pattern apparent for poverty also emerges for other income measures. Longitudinal data reveal that average income rises from young ages to middle age, but then declines from middle to old age (Crystal and Waehrer 1996; Duncan and Smith 1989). Although poverty rates reflect the experiences of the poorest people in a society, and average income reflects the experiences of middle-class people, they both show much the same pattern over the life course.

In addition to providing a less optimistic picture of changes in old age than time-series data, longitudinal data allow studies to examine the influence of class background on the distribution of income. As with retirement and health, poverty and income during old age relate closely to preretirement education, occupational status, and income.

First, education relates closely to poverty and income during old age. Among people age 65 and over, the poverty rate of those with a grade school education reaches 22 percent, whereas the poverty rate of college graduates equals only 3.5 percent (McLaughlin and Jensen 1993). Similarly, education relates as closely to income during old age as it does to income before old age (Crystal, Shea, and Krishnaswami 1992).

Second, preretirement occupational status affects poverty and income during retirement (Parnes and Less 1985). Henretta and Campbell (1976) compare a sample of men ages 55 to 64 in 1962 with a sample ages 66 to 75 in 1973. Their analysis of the two age groups uncovers nearly identical relationships between respondents' occupation and income. Although labor force status, health, marital status, and income sources change substantially during the 11 years studied, the influence of occupational status during old age remains surprisingly stable. Another study finds much the same result using a single sample of men interviewed in 1966 when they were ages 45 to 59 and in 1981 when they were ages 60 to 74 (Pampel and Hardy 1994a).

Third, income differences increase during old age (Crystal and Waehrer 1996). Again examining men ages 45 to 59 who aged to 60 to 74 during the years from 1966 to 1981, Pampel and Hardy (1994b) find that older age groups exhibit greater income differences than do middle age groups. For example, the richest 20 percent of people ages 60 to 74 own a greater portion of income than the richest 20 percent of people ages 45 to 59. Moreover, income inequality proves much higher among older retirees than among young workers.

Crystal and Shea (1990a, 1990b) similarly conclude that the equalizing influence of Social Security benefits is more than outweighed by the effect of private pensions and assets. Social insurance and means-tested programs may preserve the income of the poor, and private income and assets may preserve the income of the well-off. However, middle-income people, labeled "tweeners" by Smeeding (1990), experience financial loss relative to high- and low-income people. "Tweeners" can avoid poverty, but they do not maintain the comfortable, risk-free income they had in earlier years. As a result, differences between middle- and upper-income people increase during old age.

In some ways, public policy in the United States aims to maintain class differences in income during old age. Members of the middle class represent the largest group of recipients of benefits and the strongest political influence on policy. Having contributed substantially to Social Security during their work years, they desire benefits roughly proportional to their contributions. To satisfy these desires, public policies must limit redistribution. Private pensions tie contributions even more strongly to benefits than does Social Security. Middle-class interests thus encourage income continuity rather than income redistribution in old age.

Some contrary pressures toward equality exist as well. Currently, older people with income above $25,000 must pay taxes on their Social Security benefits, but people with income below that amount get all their benefits tax free. In the future, the high cost of medical care in old age may also require high-income older people to pay more for the Medicare benefits they receive. Many older people simply do not need normal Social Security and Medicare payments because of their high private income. Yet taxing the benefits of high-income people moves Social Security and Medicare toward means-tested programs, and means-tested programs seldom gain widespread popular support.

In the future, then, we can expect public and private pension policies to maintain class differences, and we can expect social class to remain an important component of a person's experience in old age. For example, compare the experience of two people nearing age 50 and thinking about retirement in the next decade.

ALTHOUGH ONLY 45 YEARS OLD and not yet ready to retire, Linda wonders how she will support herself. She looks forward to retirement. Having worked as a clerk at Sears for 30 years, she would like in the years to come to travel and devote more time to her hobbies of sewing, cooking, and gardening. Yet her earnings of $30,000 a year do not leave her much to save for retirement, and she does not count on Social Security: "I haven't done any more than try to invest in profit sharing. I worry a lot about it, especially about Social Security not being there." A mother at age 19 and divorced at age 31, Linda has three teenagers living with her at home, three grown sons living on their own, and four grandchildren. But she says, "I'd never live with my kids after retirement. . . . I want them to enjoy their lives. I don't want to be a burden." With a desire to retire and enjoy life, but limited options for support from work or the family, Linda's retirement looks to be difficult even with support from Social Security. Without Social Security, retirement seems impossible (Langer 1995:38–39).

COMPARED WITH LINDA, 46-year-old Jay seems better prepared for retirement. He works as a city planner in the Phoenix, Arizona, area, and his wife works as an accountant. With a combined income of more than $50,000, only one child, and careful spending habits, they feel comfortable about life after work. Like Linda, Jay does not count on Social Security. "We don't expect to collect Social Security, which is a big concern for our generation. Most of us have paid quite a bit of money into it, and I don't think it's going to be there for us." Unlike Linda, however, Jay and his wife expect to be able to live comfortably in retirement from private benefits. Jay says, "We have bonds, savings accounts, and investments. As a city employee, I have a comfortable retirement; so does my wife." The higher income and work-based retirement program give Jay and his wife advantages for retirement that Linda will not have (Langer 1995:41).

The differences between Linda and Jay reflect class divisions in society that people take for granted. However, they also define the kinds of experiences the two will have during old age. Relying on savings and private pensions, Jay will likely continue to live an affluent life in old age. Relying mostly on Social Security, Linda will likely live much more modestly in old age.

Conclusion

Social classes differ in the level of resources they enjoy, such as education, prestige, income, and power, and these differences stem in large part from advantages and disadvantages in the labor market. Higher-prestige jobs that require more education and pay higher wages than lower-prestige jobs contribute to inequality during adulthood. In old age, however, the primary source of income shifts from earnings to public and private pension benefits. Do class differences remain as important in old age as before old age? This chapter offers evidence that they do—social class distinguishes people in old age much as it does in middle age.

Because Social Security specifies a higher rate of replacement for low-income compared to high-income workers, smaller income differences might emerge in old age than in middle age. Furthermore, because Medicare provides the same health care benefits for all elderly, and SSI provides benefits for the poorest elderly, class differences in financial well-being might decline in old age. However, these sources of declining inequality in old age are balanced by sources of increasing inequality. Private pension programs, savings, and continued earnings maintain the advantages of middle- and upper-class people in old age relative to working- and lower-class people. In the end, preexisting class differences continue to influence the lives of older people.

To examine the influence of social class in old age relative to middle age, researchers rely on longitudinal rather than cross-sectional or time-series data. Following the same sample of people over time as they move from middle age to old age allows researchers to isolate the effects of aging from those related to generational differences. It also allows them to compare differences across social classes before and after the transition to retirement and old age.

These longitudinal studies show the enduring importance of social class over the last part of the life course. Those with higher education, higher-prestige occupations, and higher income before retirement generally have (a) more opportunities and incentives to keep working in old age; (b) fewer problems of poor health and disability, and longer life expectancy; and (c) lower rates of poverty and higher average income. Longitudinal data also show the variety of types of retirement, the changes in health during old age, and the overall worsening of economic status from middle age to old age. Despite these complexities, however, social class continues to influence life experiences for the elderly.

4

Race, Ethnic, and Gender
Differences in Old Age

HAVING EACH LIVED MORE THAN 100 YEARS, Sadie and Bessie Delany could look back on their lives with both pride and wonder. Born in 1889 and 1891, Sadie and Bessie grew up in North Carolina, where they suffered from the "Jim Crow" laws that segregated the races and treated blacks as second-class citizens. Their father had been born a slave but was freed at age 7 when the Civil War ended, managed to obtain schooling, and became a minister and vice principal of a local college. The sisters moved as adults to the Harlem area of New York City, where Sadie became the first black person to teach domestic science in the New York City public schools, and Bessie became the second black woman licensed to practice dentistry in New York. After successful careers, they retired nearly 40 years ago, moving together to the suburbs, staying active, and keeping close to their younger siblings, nephews, and nieces. As members of a racial minority group, they faced discrimination throughout their lives, but they managed to do well in old age (Delany and Delany 1993).

ARETHUSA FULLER, A 72-YEAR-OLD BLACK WOMAN, has lived for the past 12 years in a tiny four-room apartment on the fifth floor of a building near downtown San Francisco. A strong devotion to her Baptist religion and a belief in spiritual visions and healing give her strength to deal with her problems. Born in Mississippi, she survived racial prejudice, the death of her mother when she was 13, dropping out of school in fifth grade, and hard economic times during the Depression. She worked as a maid, but problems with her heart required early retirement. Her condition now prevents her from walking more than two blocks at a time. Although she enjoyed working, she could accumulate little for old age. She often finds herself short of food and without money to buy more groceries. Her three daughters help when they can, but they have their own financial problems. By praying and reading the Bible, Arethusa manages to stay happy despite her poor health and low income. Still, old age has been a trying time for her (Clark, Pelham, and Clark 1988:113-116).

Throughout their lives, the Delany sisters fought to better themselves in the face of discrimination and prejudice. They believed that the strength they gained in overcoming obstacles to become educated and successful helped them to deal with problems in old age. Until Bessie's death in 1995 at age 104, both had lived much longer than average, and stayed remarkably active and healthy. Not all the minority elders do as well as the Delany sisters, however. To the contrary, because of experiences with prejudice and discrimination throughout their lives, racial and ethnic minorities may find old age much worse than do majority groups. As with Arethusa Fuller, the problems brought on by minority status before old age likely continue into old age and perhaps make aging all the more difficult.

These stories raise several questions about minority status and aging. Does minority status help or hinder people in old age? Do differences between majority and minority groups before old age persist into old age? Do race and ethnic inequalities define quite different experiences in old age, as class differences do? These questions occupy those concerned with *ethnogerontology*—the combined study of aging and race-ethnicity. The same sort of questions apply to another ascribed status—gender.

The study of race, ethnicity, and gender in old age follows the logic introduced in the previous chapter to study class differences. Chapter 3 argued that, despite increased reliance on public benefits during old age, educational, occupational, and earnings backgrounds continue to influence retirement, health, and income. The combined impact of age and class defines quite different experiences of people from different backgrounds. Problems during old age strike those with fewer resources more seriously and make retirement less rewarding and satisfying.

A similar life course perspective proves useful to understand how ascriptive statuses such as race, ethnicity, and gender relate to age. Age, like race, ethnicity, and gender, is determined at birth, but unlike race, ethnicity, and gender, it changes during the lives of individuals. Therefore, we can examine how economic and social differences based on race, ethnicity, and gender change during old age. For example, aging for those of European heritage may differ from aging for African Americans, Hispanic Americans, Asian Americans, or Native Americans, and aging among men may differ from aging among women.

The combinations and possibilities for diverse experiences during old age increase quickly when considering race, ethnicity, and gender inequalities along with class inequalities. Considering this diversity leads to more than two worlds of aging—it implies dozens of worlds of aging. Much theory and research has dealt with the complexity in one of two ways. One approach simplifies the complexity by focusing on the majority group of middle-class white men, giving little systematic attention to minority groups and women. In trying to reach general conclusions about aging primarily on the basis of the majority, the approach gives minority deviations from the general patterns only secondary attention. The other approach emphasizes in-depth description of aging within a single minority group. Although much detail becomes available through such efforts, the approach makes it difficult to compare directly the numerous subgroups of older people. The research shows that aging varies by race, ethnicity, and gender, but it does not organize the diversity into a meaningful scheme.

Few seem satisfied with either of these two approaches. Some call for new approaches that can make sense of the detailed descriptive studies of minority aging but remain sensitive to the special characteristics and experiences of the minority groups (Burton, Dilworth-Anderson, and Bengtson 1992). Rather than describing one process of aging for all groups, or a separate process for each and every minority group, they recommend an approach that falls between these extremes. The approach should search for understanding of both similarities and differences in aging across groups (Stanford and Torres-Gil 1992).

With the latter approach in mind, this chapter examines how race, ethnicity, and gender influence work, health, and economic status in old age. In so doing, it provides another perspective on the diversity of experiences in old age and relates public policy to minority aging. Given the generally lower status of minority groups before old age, the study of minority aging provides another opportunity to evaluate the equalizing consequences of public policies.

Combining Disadvantaged Statuses

Because of the discrimination and prejudice it brings, membership in a racial or ethnic minority group may be viewed as a disadvantaged status; for the same reason, old age may be seen as a disadvantaged status. Discrimination in finding work and obtaining income means that these groups face special problems that younger and majority groups do not. The study of age and race-ethnicity therefore translates into the study of how disadvantaged statuses combine. On one hand, one disadvantaged status may restrain the impact of the other; the problems of old age make the problems of minority racial or ethnic status seem less important. On the other hand, one disadvantaged status may make the impact of the other all the more important; the problems of old age make the problems of minority racial or ethnic status more serious. I consider both types of combinations in turn.

Leveling of Race and Ethnic Differences

In some ways, old age may moderate or level the differences between race and ethnic groups that exist before old age. Together, race and ethnic disadvantages come to overlap with old-age disadvantages in a way that reduces the separate harm of each disadvantage. As a result, some changes in old age may reduce the gap in status between racial and ethnic groups that exists before old age.

> *ALTHOUGH 82 YEARS OLD, Wilk Peters fights to keep learning. A black man born in 1900 to a sharecropper, Wilk grew up poor in a county in Texas known for the strength of the Ku Klux Klan and racial prejudice. As a young child, he dreamed of becoming a doctor, but, when his father died, 13-year-old Wilk dropped out of the 6th grade to take over the farm chores. When his mother later remarried, he moved on his own to Tyler, Texas, where he worked in a sawmill. During these difficult times, he still dreamed of becoming a doctor. Hoping to use his modest savings for tuition, he applied to Texas College but was told to finish his high school degree first. So, he returned to sixth grade at age 23, proceeded through the other grades, received his high school diploma, and enrolled in college at age 28. Working part-time to support himself, he obtained his college degree in library science and worked as a librarian at colleges throughout the country. Remembering his thirst for knowledge when he could not attend school, Wilk kept learning. During his spare time and vacations, he mastered six languages and traveled throughout the world. Now at age 82, fully retired and free to relax, he began learning Italian to prepare for his next trip to Rome. He exhibits the same efforts to improve himself in old age that he did as a young man and adult (Franklin 1986:21-46).*

Applied to economic status, the logic of the leveling argument works as follows. The already low economic status of minority groups before old age limits the distance they can fall during old age; the already high economic status of majority white groups before old age leaves much room for a drop in economic status during old age. People near poverty before old age, who have not become accustomed to large and regular salaries, find retirement less disruptive financially than do people with high salaries in middle age (Markides and Mindel 1987).

In several ways, more deprived minority groups are used to making adjustments that can improve their quality of life in old age. They find odd jobs in their neighborhood to supplement their retirement benefits. They share resources, housing, and living costs with other relatives and friends to deal with modest income. They have already learned to live frugally on their limited resources. In relative terms, then, minority groups with previously low income lose less during old age than do majority groups with previously high income.

The same logic may apply to related outcomes, such as health. Having faced more problems of health and disability before old age, minority groups can deal better with health and social problems in old age. Indeed, the tremendous effort required to overcome two barriers—minority status and old age—may result in some benefits (Giddings 1984). The physical, economic, and social strength gained from dealing with deprivation and discrimination before old age makes people better able to deal with these problems in old age. The majority groups find the health difficulties of old age more daunting given their lack of experience with these sorts of problems at earlier ages. Relative to their health earlier in life, then, minority people do not do all that worse in old age.

Government policies contribute to this leveling of racial and ethnic differences. If government benefits are distributed more equally than private sector wages, salaries, investments, and self-employment income, it should benefit minority groups disadvantaged by discrimination in the private sector. Because the democratic nature of government programs improves the position in old age of those with lower education and lower-paying occupations, minority groups with these characteristics benefit more economically from government programs.

For example, the higher rates of return to Social Security contributions for low-income people should help minority groups that, on average, have lower earnings than do majority groups. Similarly, the universal access to medical care during old age should particularly help minority groups that cannot afford expensive private health care in old age. Finally, special means-tested programs for low-income elderly people would all help equalize the income gap between majority and minority groups.

The leveling argument also suggests that minority groups can better represent themselves in the political arena than in the market. Although discrimination exists in all aspects of social life, democratic political institutions help racial and ethnic groups that face discrimination in the private labor market. With regard to racial and ethnic differences as well as class differences, political institutions can reshape the labor market substantially to reduce inequality.

Double Jeopardy in Old Age

In other ways, old age may maintain or even amplify the differences between race and ethnic groups that exist before old age. Together, race and ethnic disadvantages combine with old-age disadvantages to make the disadvantages of elderly minority groups doubly large. Scholars refer to the combined harm of occupying two disadvantaged statuses—one based on race or ethnicity and the other on old age—as double jeopardy.

> *ALBERT SHAW, A 93-YEAR-OLD BLACK MAN, has some serious problems. He is nearly blind and hard of hearing, must use a walker to move around because of a knee ailment, and has little money. He spends most of his time sitting on a straight-back chair in his hallway looking out the window. Unable to do daily errands, he relies on his 89-year-old sister-in-law to do cooking, laundry, and cleaning for him. Friends from his church also check in on him, sometimes bring food, and take him to church on Sunday. Despite this help, problems of money make life hard. He receives Social Security and Navy retirement benefits, but they barely cover his expenses. In contrast to many others in old age, Albert did pretty well in the early years of retirement. Having worked for the government, he qualified for benefits and had a decent place to live. For each year he gets older, however, his health problems become more limiting and his money does less to cover his expenses. To live a satisfactory life at this very old age, he needs more services to deal with his blindness and his difficulty with walking, he needs more help caring for his daily needs, and he needs more money (Clark et al. 1988:153-156).*

In simple terms, double jeopardy consists of adding the disadvantages of old age to the disadvantages of minority status. For example, if minority groups on average have lower income than do majority groups, and if the elderly on average have lower income than do middle-aged people, then double jeopardy implies that the minority elders would do twice as poorly as middle-aged white people.

A more complex version suggests that the two disadvantages combine in ways that make the "whole greater than the sum of the parts." It argues that the disadvantages of old age make the disadvantages of minority groups all the greater; or, the disadvantages of minority groups make the disadvantages of old age all the greater. As a result, the problems of minority elderly appear even worse than might be expected from the separate problems of minority status and old age.

Arguments for this more complex version of double jeopardy claim that discrimination has cumulative effects over the life course (Thomas, Herring, and Horton 1994). The harm of discrimination initially shows in lower education, higher unemployment, and lower earnings among minority group youths. In turn, the loss of opportunities during youth further limits opportunities during middle age. Given their initial difficulty in the labor market as youths, minority adults find it even more difficult to obtain promotions to better jobs, earn higher salaries, accumulate assets and savings, and qualify for private and public retirement benefits. By the time of old age, minority groups have fallen farther and farther behind majority groups. If we view adulthood as a race to prepare economically for old age, then at each stage of the race, discrimination successively slows minority groups until the gap reaches its maximum in old age.

In simpler terms, the claim that "the rich get richer and the poor get poorer" reflects the idea of double jeopardy. Inequality increases over time because those who obtain initial advantages can use those advantages to obtain further advantages (Dannefer 1987). Applied to aging, early opportunities create later opportunities and increase the gap between minority and majority groups by the time people reach old age. As a result, differences between race and ethnic groups grow steadily over the life course (Grigsby 1996; O'Rand 1996).

Another way to view the extra disadvantages faced by the minority elderly focuses on the ability of people to deal with the stressful changes that occur in old age. Retirement and family change during old age can strain the resources of all people. Yet the more savings, investments, private pensions, home equity, and other assets accumulated during the work years, the more resources people have to buffer the financial threats of old age. People lacking such resources find themselves especially vulnerable to the loss of income during old age. To the extent that discrimination makes it more difficult for minority people to accumulate resources before old age, it makes the financial difficulties of old age all the more serious.

Arguments of double jeopardy imply that government programs for older people do little to reduce differences across race and ethnic groups. Because the market tends to favor majority groups relative to minority groups before old age, government policies during old age tend to do the same. Government policies invariably reflect the distribution of economic power in society and generally maintain or increase the advantages of more powerful groups. Public programs for the elderly cannot overcome the differences in resources between majority and minority groups accumulated over the work years.

Leveling and Double Jeopardy
in Race and Ethnic Differences

Studies can best evaluate the leveling and double jeopardy arguments with longitudinal data that compare race and ethnic differences in work, health, and income during both middle age and old age. Unfortunately, many studies must rely on cross-sectional data that provide detailed figures on a variety of minority groups. Still, reviewing studies using both types of data suggests that old age generally maintains race and ethnic differences that exist before old age. As a result, people of color experience old age differently from others, much the way that lower-class people experience old age differently from others.

Typically, data distinguish among whites, blacks, and white Hispanics (and less often among Asian Americans and Native Americans). Although important differences exist within each of these categories, finer measurement distinctions seldom appear in the research literature. Within the Hispanic or Latino population, for example, the aging experiences of Mexican Americans, Puerto Ricans, and Cuban Americans may differ significantly. Similarly, white ethnic groups and black regional groups differ significantly (Clarke and Neidert 1992). To keep the discussion manageable, however, I rely on broad racial and ethnic categories in reviewing the evidence on leveling and double jeopardy.

Retirement

Race influences the likelihood of work during old age. Figure 4.1 describes the rates of labor force participation of black and white men from ages 45 to 73 (Hayward, Friedman, and Chen 1996). Except at age 45, the rates for whites exceed those for blacks. At age 65, for example, 40 percent of whites participate in the labor force compared to 34 percent of blacks. However, the rates for blacks are low before old age as well—racial differences in old age continue the racial differences that exist before old age.

Because blacks are employed less than whites at most ages, it likely reflects something more than formal retirement at the oldest ages. A va-

FIGURE 4.1

Labor Force Participation Rates by Age

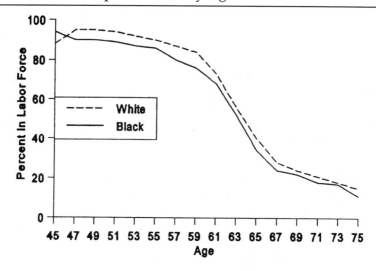

riety of forces other than desires for retirement make work in the formal labor force more difficult for blacks across all ages. The standard model of retirement assumes a shift from full-time work for a salary in middle age to leisure and receipt of a pension. Yet the low participation rates of blacks suggest that this model fits minorities poorly. Facing difficulties in finding work and accumulating pension benefits, minorities have fewer opportunities than do whites for formal retirement, and the concept of retirement has less meaning.

Gibson (1987) coins the term "the unretired-retired" to describe older African American men and women who do not have permanent, full-time jobs in old age but do not consider themselves as retired. The unretired-retired include those who have worked in low-status jobs, received low earnings, and experienced extensive periods of unemployment before old age. As a result, they do not qualify for a private pension or Social Security. Health problems and difficulty in finding work in old age keep them out of the labor force and lead them to view themselves as disabled rather than retired. Because they may work informally for money or exchange of goods, the lines between work and retirement are less clearly defined.

Two sources contribute to the unretired-retired status of many blacks in old age. First, the relatively weak attachment to the labor force means that blacks have fewer opportunities for long-term employment and more often must leave the labor force because of an inability to find work rather than a desire to retire. Second, blacks leave the labor force more often than do whites because of poor health and disability (Hayward and Grady 1990). Surveys asking older men why they are not working reveal much the same. Compared to whites, blacks more often say they retired because of poor health and less often say they retired voluntarily. The high rates of retirement for disability reflect worse health both before and during old age (Burr et al. 1996; Shea, Miles, and Hayward 1996).

Relative to studies of racial differences, studies of ethnic differences in retirement are rare. Still, Mexican Americans appear to face problems similar to those of blacks: Lower-status jobs, high risks of unemployment, and low wages make formal retirement with a private pension and Social Security benefits difficult (Zsembik and Singer 1990). Many leave the labor force because of unemployment and poor health rather than voluntary retirement, and others keep working in old age because of economic need rather than high job satisfaction. Although the field needs many more studies of retirement for ethnic groups, we can expect that the formal retirement model best fits ethnic groups from European backgrounds.

Racial and ethnic differences in work experiences before old age thus appear to critically shape experiences during old age. The less advantaged positions in the labor force of minorities during middle age makes the meaning of work and nonwork different. Although work becomes less common among all groups during old age, the causes and meaning of not working vary among race and ethnic groups. More advantaged groups retire voluntarily, could work if they wanted, and rely on public and private retirement benefits; less advantaged groups more often must retire because of poor health, cannot find jobs when they want to work, and receive less in the way of public and private retirement benefits.

Health

Studies of changes in health differences across racial and ethnic groups during old age provide some evidence for leveling arguments. For one, Gibson (1994) suggests that black handicaps in health decline during old age. The leveling of racial differences in health in old age results in part from higher rates of black mortality *before* old age, which leaves a more hardy subset of blacks *during* old age. Blacks still suffer from fewer resources and poorer medical care than do whites during old age, but blacks who survived the disadvantages before old age are better prepared than many whites to deal with the health difficulties that face all people in old age.

Also consistent with leveling arguments, mortality statistics by race reveal what some term the "cross-over phenomena" (Berkman, Singer, and Manton 1989; Manton 1982). Mortality rates for blacks exceed those for whites for ages under 80. After 80, however, death rates for whites exceed those for blacks. Drawing lines representing the death rates of blacks and whites at all ages thus shows a higher line for blacks until around age 80, when the lines cross over and whites have a higher line.

In contrast, other studies support double jeopardy arguments. In a dated but often-cited article, Dowd and Bengtson (1978) find from a study of blacks, whites, and Mexican Americans in Los Angeles that the gap in self-assessed health widens in old age. Ferraro and Farmer (1996) find no increase in the gap in self-assessed health between whites and blacks during old age, but they do find that the black disadvantage remains consistently strong. Although health declines for both blacks and whites in old age, it falls in a way that maintains the size of the preexisting gap (see also Clark and Maddox 1993).

Studies of racial differences in mortality also provide evidence for double jeopardy arguments. Because death certificates tend to overstate the age of blacks, Elo and Preston (1994) argue that mortality comparisons of blacks and whites are misleading. Overstating age at death would reduce the reported death rates of blacks at older ages and incorrectly suggest lower mortality among blacks than whites. The existence of measurement error therefore makes it more difficult to accept the leveling argument and reject the double jeopardy argument.

One longitudinal study that obtains information on age independent of death certificates indicates continued racial differences in mortality in old age. Mott and Haurin (1985) compare the likelihood of death of blacks and whites over 15 years of data and conclude that the "decline in mortality over the past fifteen years has impacted fairly equally on all segments of society; blacks and whites . . . have all apparently benefited from the general improvements in health and medical care and services available in our society" (p. 52).

A more recent study of health also relies on longitudinal data. Ferraro and Farmer (1996) examine changes in a variety of measures of health status among elderly black and white Americans over a 15-year period— from ages 50 to 64 to ages 65 to 79. The analysis of changes at the older ages finds, as expected, that blacks have poorer health than do whites. In addition, the disadvantages involve a continuation of problems from middle age to old age, suggesting that racial differences in health persist rather than decline in old age.

Smaller differences exist in mortality across ethnic groups (Rogers et al. 1996). In terms of life expectancy, Asian Americans live longest, followed by Caucasian Americans, Mexican Americans, Native Americans, and African Americans. Although Mexican Americans and Caucasian Americans have similar life expectancies, they result from different causes. Caucasian Americans die more often from diet and smoking-related diseases such as cancer and heart disease, and Mexican Americans die more often from accidents and violence associated with lower socioeconomic status. However, because studies rarely examine changes in ethnic differences from middle age to old age, they do not directly evaluate leveling and double jeopardy arguments.

In all, race and ethnic differences in health sometimes decline in old age, but not across all studies, measures, or racial and ethnic groups. Old age can also amplify preexisting health inequalities. Generalizing across the diverse findings, racial and ethnic differences appear, on average, to remain approximately the same size in old age as before old age. Racial and ethnic status remains central to health in old age as it does in middle age.

Poverty and Income

In their study of blacks, whites, and Mexican Americans in Los Angeles, Dowd and Bengtson (1978) also examine economic differences. Comparing the size of income differences across race and ethnic groups for people ages 45 to 64 and for people 65 and over, they find that the gap in income across the groups increases with old age. In support of the double jeopardy argument, they claim that old age expands income differences that existed across the race and ethnic groups before old age.

In a review of other evidence, however, Markides, Liang, and Jackson (1990) argue the opposite: "There is consistent evidence that health and income differentials decline in old age between blacks and whites . . . but not consistently so between Hispanics and other whites" (p. 115). They note in particular that Dowd and Bengtson rely on data for one time point. A more precise comparison would follow the same group of people over time and compare changes in income as they grow older.

To illustrate this type of life course analysis more precisely, Table 4.1 presents figures on poverty rates from government surveys done in 1982

TABLE 4.1

Percentage below Poverty by Age and Race-Ethnicity

	1982			1992		
Age	White	Black	Hispanic	White	Black	Hispanic
45 to 54	7.9	21.9	18.9			
55 to 64	8.8	28.7	20.1	8.6	24.0	23.3
65 to 74				8.6	29.6	19.5

and 1992 (U.S. Bureau of the Census 1982, 1992). For 1982, the table shows the percentage of whites, blacks, and Hispanics below the poverty line in two late-middle-age groups: 45 to 54 and 55 to 64. For 1992, the table shows the percentage of whites, blacks, and Hispanics below the poverty line for the same age groups 10 years later and 10 years older: 55 to 64 and 65 to 74. Comparing people 45 to 54 in 1982 with people 55 to 64 in 1992, and comparing people 55 to 64 in 1982 with people 65 to 74 in 1992 contrasts the same groups of people (excepting those who die or migrate) at middle age and old age.

Note two initial findings from these figures. One, poverty generally rises with old age among all the groups; people 55 to 64 generally have higher poverty rates than do people 45 to 54, and people 65 to 74 generally have higher poverty rates than do people 55 to 64. Two, regardless of the age group, poverty occurs more often among blacks and Hispanics than among whites. These facts simply demonstrate that both race-ethnicity and old age, by producing higher poverty rates, represent disadvantaged statuses. However, the separate disadvantaged statuses do not reveal if they combine in ways consistent with leveling or double jeopardy.

The high rates of poverty among Hispanics shown by these figures partly reflect the difficulties faced by immigrants when they reach old age. Because of the kinds of low-status, low-pay jobs they often take in the United States, immigrants often do not qualify for public or private retirement benefits.

REFUGEES FROM CUBA IN THEIR LATE 60s, Alfonso and Elizabeth Gutierrez do not qualify for Social Security benefits. Although they worked seasonally for many years picking tomatoes, they did not make sufficient contributions to qualify for benefits. They now live on Supplemental Security Income (SSI) and Elizabeth's occasional part-time work in a nearby factory. They live in a four-room cinder-block house with a leaky roof on the outskirts of Miami. The mortgage, taxes, and insurance for the house, as well as utility expenses for water, gas, and electricity, take up 62 percent of their income. They need to repair the house, buy medicine for Alfonso's emphysema, and repay some missed mortgage payments, but they have no extra money. Mrs. Gutierrez says, "I did not think being old like this would be so hard" (Margolis 1990:84).

FREDESVINDA MARMOL ALSO ENTERED the United States as an immigrant, but she came from the Dominican Republic in the Caribbean 30 years ago. Although she worked in a factory in New York City until her eyesight failed, she never became a citizen of the United States because she did not know enough English to pass the citizenship test. Now 80 years old, the victim of near blindness, a recent stroke, and the early stages of Alzheimer's disease, her sole source of income comes from SSI. She now worries that efforts to cut noncitizens from the rolls of SSI will leave her without any income at all. Becoming a citizen, the only sure way to avoid losing SSI benefits, will be difficult in her case (Harpaz 1997).

Given the racial and ethnic differences in poverty, the next step in the analysis requires a comparison of how the *differences* change as people grow older. Among people 45 to 54 in 1982, the gap between whites and blacks equals 14 percent, and the gap between whites and Hispanics equals 11 percent. Among the same group of people ages 55 to 64 in 1992, the gap between blacks and whites equals 15.4 percent, and the gap between whites and Hispanics equals 14.7 percent. The increases from 14.0 to 15.4 percent and from 11.0 to 14.7 percent indicate a tendency for racial and ethnic differences in poverty to increase with aging.

Among people ages 55 to 64 in 1982, the gap between blacks and whites equals 19.9 percent, and the gap between whites and Hispanics equals 11.3 percent. Among people 65 to 74 in 1992, the gap between blacks and whites equals 21.0 percent, and the gap between whites and Hispanics equals 10.9 percent. The change from 19.9 to 21.0 percent and from 11.3 to 10.9 percent indicates a slight increase in the difference between blacks and whites but a slight decrease in the difference between whites and Hispanics. Although available figures are not strictly comparable (and not included in Table 4.1), poverty among people age 75 and over in 1992 likewise shows stability in racial and ethnic differences in poverty rates in late old age.

A conservative interpretation of these results would conclude that racial and ethnic differences in poverty do not consistently or strongly increase or decrease. Small increases in racial and ethnic differences sometimes emerge, but in at least one case, a decrease occurs. Averaged across all the comparisons, the racial and ethnic differences in poverty rates remain much the same. As with work and health, economic differences among races and ethnic groups continue to influence the experience of old age. Given the lower income of minority groups before old age, only a drastic change in the nature of public programs could eliminate inequality. Because both public and private pensions depend on previous earnings, minorities have lower retirement benefits than do others. They are also more likely to be out of the labor force and disabled—both conditions that would harm their economic status during old age.

Gender and Age

Like race and ethnicity, gender defines advantaged and disadvantaged positions in society. Compared to men, women work less often because of family and domestic duties. Furthermore, women in the paid labor force typically have low-status clerical, sales, and service jobs; these jobs offer low pay, limited pension benefits, and high turnover. When women do obtain higher-status professional and managerial jobs, they experience fewer promotion opportunities, less authority and power on the job, and lower salaries than do men. Such differences result less from biological characteristics than from sex stereotypes about the roles of men and women, discrimination by employers, and different patterns of socialization of men and women (Reskin and Padavic 1994).

Feminists suggest that gender inequality in the modern labor force reflects larger structures of male privilege. Because men have maintained power within the family in traditional societies, they also control resources within the modern economy. Their privilege shows in the pressures exerted to segregate women into lower-status, "female" occupations and to hold them responsible for unpaid family and child-rearing duties. The end result is to maintain the resource advantages of male workers. These processes of gender domination continue throughout the life course and significantly affect the experience of aging.

How does the disadvantaged status of women combine with the disadvantaged status of old age? The same sort of leveling and double jeopardy arguments about racial and ethnic statuses in old age also apply to gender. Indeed, one can extend the double jeopardy argument into triple or multiple jeopardy by jointly considering the disadvantages of gender, race-ethnicity, and old age. However, to keep things manageable, I focus now on gender and age alone.

According to the leveling arguments, the loss of resources experienced in old age proves greater for men than for women. As a result, inequality between women and men shrinks during old age. During middle age, gender differences in labor force experiences, wages and salaries, and public and private pension contributions create a large gap in the independent resources available to men and women. Although married women can rely on the resources of their spouse, they accumulate fewer resources for themselves should divorce or widowhood occur. During old age, however, public programs moderate the market disadvantages of women. Social Security benefits for elderly women whose spouse has died or who do not qualify on their own for normal benefits help support elderly women without other resources. Also, Supplemental Security Income and Medicare disproportionately go to women.

According to gender-based arguments of double jeopardy, the loss of resources experienced in old age differs little across genders or proves worse for women than for men. As a result, inequality between women and men stays constant or grows during old age. Double jeopardy arguments claim that the lack of labor force experience, low wages and salaries, and limited public and private pension contributions of women before old age make it extremely difficult to deal with the financial and health problems of old age. Having the opportunity to accumulate more resources in better paying and longer term jobs, men are better prepared for the problems of old age. Although married women can rely on the resources of their spouse, the growing number of divorced and widowed women face special problems in old age (Holden and Kuo 1996). Public programs may moderate some of the problems of old age for older women with benefits from means-tested programs, deceased spouses, or insurance policies, but these income sources cannot fully overcome the financial hardship stemming from the limited access of many women to the labor force before old age (Burkhauser, Duncan, and Hauser 1994; Meyer 1990).

Because they live longer on average than men, women spend more time in old age and confront greater physical and financial challenges than do men. Consistent with double jeopardy, survivorship can bring severe problems.

BOTH MRS. BASCOM AND MRS. ALLEN come from prosperous upper-middle-class families, but now, having lived until their 90s, they must adapt *to disabilities that leave both of them housebound. Mrs. Bascom has outlived two husbands and two daughters, and she has little contact with her grand-children or great-grandchildren. Constant pain from severe arthritis makes it difficult for her to keep up friends, leave her house, or even get out of bed. She speaks only with the people hired to take care of her and with her lawyer, who manages her dwindling resources. Depressed, anxious, and hostile, she asks, "Why has God let me live so long?" Mrs. Allen must brave the same sort of physical and financial problems as Mrs. Bascom, but she has remained cheery and resourceful. Although she suffers also from severe arthritis, a cane, walker, and wheelchair help her get around in the senior housing center where she lives. She relies on hired help, her daughter, and friends who visit to keep her apartment clean and stocked with food. With subsidized housing and $800 a month in income, she manages to get by financially. Old age has demanded that she make enormous adjustments in her life, but her positive attitude helps her deal with them (Johnson and Barer 1997:9-10).*

In evaluating competing arguments of double jeopardy and leveling as applied to gender, I briefly review evidence on work, health, and income differences between males and females in old age. First, despite similarly low rates of employment in old age, men and women experience the process of retirement differently. All too often, however, studies of retirement concentrate on men because they more often follow the ideal pattern of an abrupt shift from a long-term work career to complete and formal retirement (Calasanti 1993). In contrast, women more often enter old age having left the labor force for extended periods to raise children and having worked at jobs with low status, pay, and fringe benefits. Although many women reenter the labor force after childbearing and before old age, pension rules favor those with continuous and lengthy employment, and women enter old age less able to formally retire with adequate pension benefits (Quadagno 1988). Many women retire simultaneously with, and rely on the higher pension benefits of, their husbands. However, the increasingly large number of divorced and widowed women makes the lack of full-time employment during the adult years a special problem in old age.

Second, gender differences in health present a puzzle: Although women outlive men, they also experience more health problems and disability. On one hand, the 1990 life expectancy for women is 79 years, whereas life expectancy for men is 72 years (U.S. Bureau of the Census 1994:87). On the other hand, women experience more physical limitations, disabilities, and sickness during old age than do men. For example, of those age 70 and over, 24 percent of women compared to 15 percent of men have disabilities (Crimmins et al. 1997:S63).

Women experience more health problems because they live longer. In addition, however, even compared to men of the same age, women experience more health problems. Where men tend to suffer more often from diseases of the heart that produce death without a prolonged period of disability, women tend to suffer more often from diseases such as arthritis and osteoporosis that produce disability rather than death. As a result, women spend a larger proportion of their old age as disabled (Crimmins et al. 1994). In terms of physical problems, the longer lives of women contribute to double jeopardy.

Third, gender differences in income and poverty show an increasing disadvantage of women relative to men. Table 4.2 presents poverty rates for men and women before and after old age (U.S. Bureau of the Census 1982, 1992). In 1982, females ages 45 to 54 have a poverty rate 2.8 percent higher than for males of the same age. Ten years later, in 1992, at ages 55 to 64, females have a poverty rate 4.0 percent higher than that for males. Although not a large increase, it shows higher poverty for older women relative to men. In 1982, females ages 55 to 64 have a poverty rate 4.3 percent higher than that for men. Ten years later, in 1992, at ages 65 to 74, females have a poverty rate 4.6 percent higher. This suggests less of a change in the poverty gap between older men and women: Relative poverty levels remain nearly constant over this 10-year period.

Widowhood and the longer life expectancy of women contribute to poverty among older women. Along with bringing personal adjustment difficulties, widowhood has economic consequences. Because private and public pension benefits for survivors seldom match those for the (typically male) recipient, widowhood lowers the financial status of women (Holden and Smock 1991). In fact, many widows past retirement age shift directly from above poverty income to below poverty income. For example, at ages 75 and over, the poverty rate among women rises to 19.8 percent (compared to 12.7 percent for women ages 65 to 74).

Familism

Compared with white men, racial and ethnic minorities and women experience more serious financial and health problems during old age. One response to these problems, especially for widowed or divorced people, involves shared living arrangements. Living with adult children, other relatives, or nonrelatives provides a way for elderly people in need to share economic resources and obtain help with tasks made difficult by health problems. If economic and health problems prove greater for mi-

TABLE 4.2

Percentage below Poverty by Age and Gender

Age	1982		1992	
	Male	Female	Male	Female
45 to 54	8.0	10.8		
55 to 64	8.3	12.6	8.2	12.2
65 to 74			8.1	12.7

norities and women, then they may be most likely to live with other family members.

To distinguish the strength of ties of people to their family, the concept of familism proves helpful. *Familism* is defined as values emphasizing the needs of the family over the rights of the individual (Gratton 1987). It produces strong ties among family members of different generations and may result in extended living arrangements in which grandparents, parents, children, and other relatives share households.

Does familism show in the living arrangements of minorities? According to census data on minority elders, it does (Himes, Hogan, and Eggebeen 1996). Blacks, Asians, and Hispanics are more likely than whites to live with family members other than their spouse, and less likely to live in institutions, alone, or with a spouse only. Not only do minority elders often share housing with adult children, elderly siblings, or cousins, they also share households with nonrelatives. Finally, racial and ethnic minority groups less often resort to nursing home care for elderly family members and more often attempt to care for them informally (Belgrave, Wykle, and Choi 1993).

Himes et al. (1996:45) present the percentage of people age 60 and over living with relatives other than their spouse for five racial and ethnic groups. Figure 4.2 presents these percentages in the form of a bar chart. Only 21 percent of white elderly people share living arrangements with relatives other than their spouse. Yet for all the other groups, the percentages are nearly twice as high. About 59 percent of elderly Asian Americans, 49 percent of Hispanic Americans, 43 percent of African Americans, and 39 percent of Native Americans live with other relatives.

Despite the diversity of experiences within racial and ethnic groups, Himes et al. (1996) find similarities among the various Hispanic ethnic groups. Although Mexican Americans are slightly more likely to live

FIGURE 4.2

Living with Other Relatives

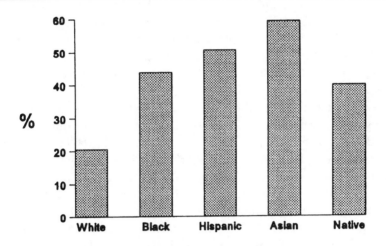

with other relatives than are Puerto Ricans and Cubans Americans, the differences remain small. Among Asian Americans, those from Vietnamese, Korean, and Chinese backgrounds are more likely than are those from Japanese backgrounds to share living arrangements with other relatives. Again, however, differences across ethnic groups appear more important than do differences within ethnic groups.

Economic Sources of Familism

These patterns of family ties stem in part from economic need. Shared living arrangements allow people to combine their resources and provide informal help to one another. A history of discrimination and economic deprivation has, in particular, produced diverse family structures among minority groups as a means of survival in difficult circumstances. Consistent with this economic explanation, studies demonstrate that the relatively low income of minority group members contributes to the complex patterns of family structure (Angel and Tienda 1982; Mutran 1985). Relatively low income of minority groups may also lead to living with non-relatives—those treated as kin even though blood ties do not exist (Stoller and Gibson 1994).

This picture of extended families as a refuge of minority elders from economic deprivation may not, however, fully reflect the circumstances of elderly people (Silverstein and Waite 1993). Although multigeneration households may well emerge to deal with economic problems, they may also respond more to problems of younger family members than of elderly family members. Elderly parents in extended households may have to provide financial support for adult children, maintain the household for other members, and care for grandchildren. As Gratton (1987) argues, multigeneration living arrangements may do more to burden elderly members than they do to relieve the burden.

Exaggerated claims of the economic benefits of extended families to elderly minority members may also result in misleading policy claims. If shared living arrangements help deal with financial problems of elderly minorities brought about by meager retirement benefits, then some might conclude that minority groups do not require improved public benefits, or that families rather than the government provide a better means of protection during old age. However, if shared living arrangements do not prove so ideal, it emphasizes the need for more universal and generous benefits during old age. Sufficient public support would allow most minority elders to enjoy independent and autonomous living arrangements.

Cultural Sources of Familism

In addition to economic circumstances, patterns of minority living arrangements also reflect value differences in familism. Although values may originate in economic circumstances of groups, they can continue to influence behavior of group members even after economic circumstances change (Burr and Mutchler 1993, 1994). Numerous studies cite examples of norms within minority groups that emphasize the duties of adult children to care for and respect elderly parents (Gelfand 1994; Hennessy and John 1995; Markides and Mindel 1987; Palmore 1984).

> *THE DELANY SISTERS, Sadie and Bessie, never married and lived with each other after they moved to New York City. Their older brother, Hap, owned an apartment house where he and his family lived upstairs. Sadie and Bessie lived in one apartment on the second floor, their sisters Julia and Laura lived in another apartment on the second floor, and their other brother Sam lived next door. When their father died, they moved their mother to New York City to live with them. Eventually, when Bessie was 59, she retired from dentistry to take care of her 90-year-old mother. Sadie kept working as a teacher until she could get a pension. Bessie says she did not think twice about giving up her job to take care of her mother. She and Sadie put them-*

selves in charge of their mother's happiness. The other children also fussed over her: When the mother complained to one son that he did not visit her often enough, he made sure he came every single day from then on, sending flowers or calling when he was sick. In Bessie's words, "Mama was the queen bee" until she died at the age of 95 (Delany and Delany 1993:176-180).

In addition to relying on family help, as the Delanys did, African Americans also rely on nonkin, community, and church support for aiding needy elderly people. Similarly, compared to whites, Japanese Americans and Mexican Americans attempt to handle crises within families rather than through public service agencies and formal organizations. Among Native American communities such as the Pueblos, norms that emphasize family harmony and interdependency likewise place responsibility for older kin within the family.

Norms of familism may stem from agrarian backgrounds of many ethnic groups that have recently immigrated into the United States. Traditional family norms and respect for the elderly emerge most strongly in rural communities, where the family remains the dominant social institution and the dominant source of financial and social support for members of all ages. Even after migration to more urbanized settings, the cultural norms that developed in rural communities endure. The norms may weaken among generations born in new settings but remain in some form even after two or three generations in the United States (Markides and Mindel 1987). Thus, Angel et al. (1996) find that a larger fraction of foreign-born Mexican Americans than native-born Mexican Americans currently live with their children and state that they would like to live with their children if they could no longer support themselves.

These arguments reflect a version of modernization theory applied to the elderly. Cowgill and Holmes (1972) argued several decades ago that older people enjoy high status in traditional societies because their accumulated wisdom, experience, and knowledge prove useful when things change slowly and people employ traditional solutions to social problems. In modern societies, however, changes reduce the special social position of elderly people. Migration and urbanization separate family members geographically when children live in different towns and countries from their older parents. Scientific and technological advancement make the knowledge of older people outdated. Mass education of children in formal schools replaces the passing down of traditions from older generations to newer generations. All of these changes brought about by modernization weaken the respected position of elderly people and their dominant role in the family. Yet recent ethnic immigrants to the United

States from traditional cultures in Latin America or Asia may uphold the traditional family values that they bring with them.

Bradshaw and Wallace (1996) describe the strong ties among family members in primarily rural communities in Africa. "Divorce is rare; retirement homes are virtually nonexistent as old people live with their relatives; and families and villages take care of each other" (p. 60). To illustrate, they tell a story about a Zambian friend of theirs named Joseph Taguma:

> HAVING MOVED TO LONDON, Joseph rented a home of "a middle-aged woman whose mother lived alone across the city. One day the mother continued to call her daughter and, since the daughter was out of the house, Joseph continued to answer the phone. On the fifth call in under two hours, our friend finally asked, 'Madame, is there something I can help you with?' The elderly women replied, 'No, I'm just so lonely.' Having just arrived in London after living in Africa his entire life, our friend could not understand how any elderly person could feel this way. . . . He interpreted the situation from his own culture, where elderly people are (1) deeply respected and (2) never without the company of other family members. . . . Africans see Westerners as too quick to dispose of an older and wiser generation" (Bradshaw and Wallace 1996:60).

Critics note that the excessively broad contrast between two types of societies—traditional and modern—misses the diverse positions of the elderly within each type of society. The contrast also ignores many differences in the position of the elderly across diverse immigrant ethnic groups. Thus, one can easily find exceptions to the broad claims of modernization theory. As Blakemore and Boneham (1994) note, "Trying to squeeze a wide variety of examples of change into a 'tradition-to-modernity' framework [is] a task rather like driving a large truck into a narrow cul-de-sac" (p. 31). Nevertheless, the family patterns and family values of racial and ethnic groups in the United States do prove consistent in some ways with the distinction between tradition and modernization. Without accepting fully the modernization framework or forcing all ethnic group experiences into one pattern, scholars can use its basic insight to inform their thinking about minority aging.

However, the same concern expressed about exaggerated claims of the economic benefits of extended families applies to cultural arguments as well. Although minority groups may desire more strongly to live with other family members, we should not idealize those arrangements. If the cultural values may ultimately stem from economic deprivation, higher economic resources may allow minority elderly to live independently and autonomously.

Conclusion

This chapter offers an additional way to describe the varied experiences and meanings of old age by considering differences in aging across racial, ethnic, and gender groups. A review of existing studies and a presentation of some simple statistics on minority aging illustrate the complexity of the changes from middle age to old age. In some cases, old age seems to expand existing inequalities, whereas in other cases, it seems to reduce them. A conservative interpretation of the varied results makes this simple point: Old age generally maintains race, ethnic, and gender differences.

Race and ethnic minorities do worse in terms of work, health status, and economic resources than do majority groups in old age. However, because minorities do worse in middle age as well, old age seems to maintain the preexisting inequality. Inequality between men and women persists into old age. Because women live longer than men, they face more years without a marriage partner, and because they lack the labor force experience and accumulated pension benefits of men, they face additional financial risk during old age. Furthermore, their longer life expectancy makes women more vulnerable to physical disabilities and health problems before death. Different family structures limit the problems faced by minority groups and women in old age but cannot eliminate them altogether.

One could easily refine and complicate these conclusions about multiple race, ethnic, and gender groups before and during old age. Important class differences exist within race, ethnic, and gender groups in old age, and more detailed studies try to consider the combined influences of class, race, ethnicity, and gender. Still, by highlighting connections between age and minority status, scholarship in ethnogerontology emphasizes the need to avoid attributing the characteristics of white, male, middle-class elders to other groups.

5

Old Age Support in
Comparative Perspective

*IN 1989, MARGARET BROCK gave this testimony to a Special Committee
on Aging of the U.S. Senate:*

> *My husband and I believed we had taken care of the future—so-called retirement.
> Shortly after his retirement, I began to notice a strangeness in his behavior. To
> shorten this, the strangeness was the beginning of Alzheimer's disease. I managed
> to take care of him at home for over a year. Then he became violent, incontinent,
> and didn't know where he was. He was past 80 years old when he worsened to this
> point. I was 16 years younger, but a severe arthritic. It finally became impossible
> to cope with this situation. (U.S. Senate 1990:4-5)*

To put him in a health care facility, she found that

> *the first month has to be paid in advance, plus transportation to the facility. All
> in all, it was $2000 before he was even admitted. Then came the extras—diapers,
> medications, etc. You are looking at approximately $2300 a month. And it went
> up to $2600, by the way. . . . This went on for 2 years until I felt like a drowning
> person must feel. (U.S. Senate 1990:4-5)*

*AT ABOUT THE SAME TIME, the experiences of an elderly Swedish cou-
ple worked out quite differently. Erik, a retired army colonel, also developed
Alzheimer's disease. After caring for him as best she could, his wife, Kristen,
moved him into a nursing home, where he would receive full-time care. Yet
because of government programs, the cost to her was only $274 per month
(Moseley 1993).*

*"THE EUROPEAN KNOWS that if he gets sick he can go to a good hospital
and it won't bankrupt him," says Paul Breuer, a former stockbroker and current owner of a small rare book and manuscript business in Germany. Despite a tax rate approaching 60 percent of his income, he does not complain.
He says that because of high taxes, a European "knows his child will get a
good education. He knows if his old parent gets sick or they need someone to*

give them a bath or take them out for a walk, they're protected. To Americans, these can be financially disastrous. But we don't fear them. That is why we keep paying. That is why we say, we don't like it but the taxes are necessary." Richard Reid, A German economist, explains the willingness of Europeans to pay high taxes now in exchange for government protection this way: "There is a perception in Europe that if you live beyond your means, that is bad. In the United States it is more growth mentality" (Nash 1995:10).

HIGH SPENDING FOR SOCIAL WELFARE programs can bring problems, however. Having the largest percentage of the population over age 65 in Europe and perhaps the world, Sweden faces enormous costs and high taxes to provide generous benefits in old age. Mats Thorslund, an expert on aging at Stockholm University in Sweden, says,

> *Sweden will not be that different from other countries in the future. We have been used to having our kids in day-care centers and old people cared for by the system, leaving the rest of us free to do whatever we want. But the party is over.*

Although politicians disagree vigorously over the kinds of changes to make, most agree that the European nations cannot continue with the kind of expensive programs they have had until now (Moseley 1993).

Policies concerning nursing home care in both the United States and Sweden have changed in the past few years. Older citizens in the United States no longer must "spend down" all their assets to get subsidized nursing home care, and older citizens in Sweden must pay a larger portion of their nursing home costs than in the past. Still, as illustrated by the stories above, European nations traditionally have provided more to their citizens and required them to pay more in the way of taxes to receive the generous benefits. Far from typical, old-age policies in the United States and the taxes to pay for them contrast markedly from other high-income, democratic nations.

At one time, scholars expected few differences in social policies across high-income nations. Many predicted that the common technology of economically advanced nations would produce similar economic and social institutions (e.g., Kerr 1983). Applied to pensions, the general argument notes that the demands of industry for young, recently educated, and geographically mobile workers created employment problems for older, sick, and less skilled workers. To meet the needs of this vulnerable population, governments came to offer public pension support. Just as all industrial nations experienced these employment problems, all industrial nations would develop similar public programs to deal with them.

Research in the past several decades has rejected claims of similarity in old-age support. To the contrary, even if common problems of supporting a growing retired population face all high-income nations, they have responded with differing solutions to the common problems. The variety of programs that have emerged reflect political and social differences across the economically similar nations. This chapter examines the varied national characteristics of public pension programs and the political and social environments that produce program differences in North America, Europe, and Japan.

Examining policies for old age in other nations provides a useful perspective to help understand the special characteristics of old-age support in the United States. Without knowledge of the types of policies provided by other nations, we have only a limited idea of how our own policies affect social life and how social life might differ under other systems. With a cross-national perspective on the variety of programs in other nations, it becomes difficult to view the problems of old age as the inevitable result of biological and physiological changes.

Despite the broad focus of this chapter, remember that national policies shape the lives and social experiences of individuals. For elderly people, the pension system in a nation determines the resources available to them, the degree of inequality in old age, and the overall well-being of a group vulnerable to social and economic problems. For other age groups, the pension system in a nation determines the assistance that young families can expect in supporting their older relatives, the taxes workers must pay, and the kind of old age that adults can expect when they grow older.

Comparing Public Pension Systems

In comparing national differences in public old-age policy, scholars distinguish three types of rules for the allotment of public pension benefits (Myles 1984; Palme 1990). First, *universal or citizenship entitlement* provides basic benefits—usually in the form of an identical or flat-rate payment—to individuals or family members above a certain age as a right of citizenship or residency. Qualifying for benefits does not depend on work history, previous contributions, or income, and funding comes from general tax revenues rather than from special pension funds. Because of the potentially high costs of universal pension programs, payments remain small but provide a floor on which other programs can build.

Second, *earnings or social insurance entitlement* bases eligibility on wage and payroll contributions made before old age or retirement. In principle, benefits based on previous contributions represent a form of social insurance—the payments made to retirees should correspond to the money put in during the work years. As in the United States, however, programs deviate from strict insurance principles. Current workers make contributions to support current retirees under the expectation that future workers will make contributions to support future retirees. Yet having made previous contributions becomes a qualifying condition for receiving benefits later in life.

Third, *need-based or means-tested entitlement* provides benefits to those whose economic resources fall below a standard typically based on subsistence needs. Means-tested pension benefits target the most needy in old age, usually those otherwise not covered by citizenship or insurance programs. Sometimes, programs provide special benefits to groups commonly in need, such as widows. Because these types of benefits take the form of social assistance, the payments tend to remain low relative to social insurance benefits, and they go to only a small part of the aged population.

To a large extent, nations mix their reliance on the different types of entitlement rules. Nations that began with universal systems added earnings-based supplements, and nations that originally enacted earnings-based systems have added universal benefits or some form of need-based benefit. Similar changes occur in the mix of public and private systems. Nations that have traditionally relied on private systems have increasingly expanded public system benefits, particularly for those without private pensions. Nations traditionally relying on public system benefits have increasingly expanded private benefits, particularly for high-income workers wanting more return on their contributions than that offered by public systems.

Despite the tendency to mix the criteria for eligibility for pension benefits, nations differ substantially in the primary criterion they use. As a result, important national differences exist in old-age support that relate to the size of benefit payments, coverage of the elderly population, and inequality in the distribution of benefits. The next sections compare these dimensions of old-age support across the high-income nations and relate the dimensions to the dominant criteria for eligibility under the program.

National Levels of Spending

One straightforward way to compare national differences in old-age support involves examining total spending levels for programs for the elderly (International Labour Office 1989). Because pension spending usually represents the largest source of public income for older people, it
represents a good starting point for making national comparisons. To
compare nations with different standards of living, however, the figures
on pension spending need to adjust for national income. Furthermore,
because nations differ in the population eligible for pensions, the figures
on spending should also adjust for the size of the elderly population.

To begin, consider the populations in 18 high-income nations in 1990.
Figure 5.1 depicts the percentage of the population age 65 and over for
these nations. Compared to other nations, these high-income nations
have relatively old populations. Still, much variation exists even within
this subset. The nation with the most elderly, Sweden, has 17.5 percent of
its population age 65 and over. The nations with the fewest elderly, Australia, New Zealand, and Japan, have 10.5 percent of their populations
age 65 and over. Sweden will spend more on pensions in part because it
has so many more potential recipients. The United States, with 12.1 percent of the population age 65 and over in 1986, falls near the bottom.

To obtain a measure of pension spending per older person, I divide
pension expenditures from the International Labour Office by the number of elderly people and divide this figure by the gross domestic product
(GDP) to adjust for both age structure and the standard of living. The end
result equals a measure of the average pension benefit per older person
as a percentage of the standard of living. Figure 5.2 presents this measure
in the form of a bar chart, with the larger bars indicating more generous
pension benefits.

The mean of this measure indicates that pension benefits per older
person average about 59 percent, or nearly two-thirds of the typical standard of living. Based on public benefits alone, pensions do not fully bring
recipients up to the average living standard of the society as a whole.
More importantly, the benefit per older person reveals huge variation
across countries. The United States offers public pension benefits equal
to 35 percent of the standard of living, obviously requiring that elderly
people have private pension or family sources of support. The Netherlands offers benefits equal to 92 percent of the standard of living (with
Italy and New Zealand also offering high benefits).

One might expect that those nations with low levels of public pension spending for the elderly would instead have high levels of private

FIGURE 5.1

Population Age 65 and Over

pension spending. That proves true to some extent. Rein and Rain-water (1986) compute spending for private as well as public pensions for a subset of these nations in 1980. They find that the greater the public spending, the lower the private spending, and that the lower the public spending, the greater the private spending. However, they also find that public spending levels in all cases exceed private spending levels. Therefore, adding up public and private spending into a measure of total pension support fails to change the ranking of nations based on the levels of public support alone. Adding private support moves the low-ranking nations, such as Japan and the United States, closer to the high-ranking nations, such as Germany and the Netherlands, but nevertheless does not change the overall ordering. Measured in any of several ways, the United States spends less on pensions than nearly all other high-income nations.

One might also expect that those nations spending less on pensions might spend more for other types of programs in support of the elderly, such as health care, food and housing benefits, or nursing home care. In fact, the opposite occurs. Those nations spending more on public pen-

FIGURE 5.2

Pension Benefit per Aged Person

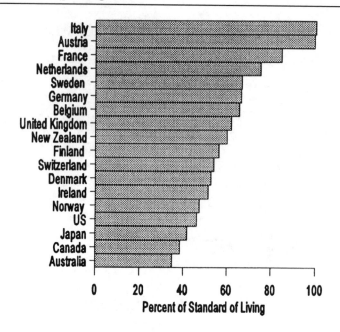

sions generally spend more on other programs benefiting older people. Rather than competing, with high spending for one program meaning low spending for another, the programs generally coincide in levels of support: High spending for one means high spending for the others. Thus, we can speak of nations as relatively generous or less generous with regard to general old-age support and specific public pension support.

Public Pension Rights

The level of pension spending misses something important in social protection during old age. It only partially reflects the coverage of the population by the program and the equality in the distribution of the benefits. Usually, the more people who qualify for public pension benefits, the higher the spending for pensions. Yet some nations may cover all or nearly all of the aged population but provide relatively small benefits; other nations may cover a relatively small part of the aged population but provide high benefits. Despite similar total spending, the nations making benefits more widely available will do more to reduce poverty and inequality in old age. Generous benefits, if available to only part of the aged population, may do little to help those most in need.

Differences across nations in pension system characteristics such as the coverage of the population and the equality of benefit distribution relate closely to the rules for eligibility. Systems based on citizenship entitlement provide for the widest coverage, and payment in the form of a flat-rate benefit most promotes equality in old age. Systems based on wage contributions made during adulthood produce less-than-universal coverage. Workers must contribute to the system for a number of years— sometimes up to 30 or 40 years—before they become eligible for benefits. Criteria based on means-tests may help raise the income of the poor closer to income of the nonpoor but give benefits to only a small portion of the population.

John Myles (1984) has classified the high-income nations according to the percentage of the population over age 65 covered by public pension systems. Most nations cover 100 percent of the population with some form of basic benefit. Canada and Sweden, for instance, cover all citizens (and even noncitizens who have lived in the country long enough) with a basic pension benefit. Germany, Austria, Belgium, and France cover approximately 75 percent of citizens, and the United States covers approximately 65 percent of citizens. The United States falls low on the ranking of pension spending in part because it does not cover people who have not made contributions for a specified period of time.

Along with coverage, nations can differ in the equality of the benefits. Inequality in pension spending would show in a large gap between the minimum benefit of a low-income worker and the maximum benefit of a high-income worker; equality would show in minimum and maximum benefits of similar size. To measure this inequality, Palme (1990) calculates the pension benefit of a single person who made the minimum contributions necessary to receive benefits. He also calculates the pension benefit of a single person who made the maximum contributions. Taking these benefits as a percentage of the after-tax wages of an average production worker, he measures how well pension benefits replace average wages. Comparing the replacement rate for minimum and maximum benefits shows the degree of inequality in pension systems.

Table 5.1 lists the minimum and maximum replacement rates for countries in 1985 from Palme (1990:93). The next column divides the maximum by the minimum replacement rate. The higher this ratio, the

TABLE 5.1

National Differences in Measures of Public Pension Rights

Nation	Minimum Benefit[a]	Maximum Benefit[a]	Maximum/ Minimum
Australia	100	100	1.00
Netherlands	100	100	1.00
New Zealand	100	100	1.00
Denmark	94	100	1.07
Ireland	86	100	1.17
Canada	85	100	1.18
Norway	70	115	1.64
United Kingdom	72	117	1.64
France	84	143	1.70
United States	53	100	1.89
Switzerland	54	105	1.95
Sweden	62	133	2.15
Belgium	50	117	2.35
Austria	70	232	3.31
Japan	21	148	7.09
Italy	27	218	8.13
Finland	70	—	—
Germany	—	262	—

a. As a percentage of average earnings.

greater the inequality in benefits. Australia, the Netherlands, and New Zealand provide the same replacement rate for both workers, resulting in a ratio of one and equal distribution of benefits. Denmark and Canada have ratios close to one. Austria, Italy, and France have the greatest ratio and the largest gap between low-income and high-income workers during retirement. The United States falls in the middle.

Public Pension Programs and Inequality

Because pension systems vary in the equality of benefits, they might also differ in the consequences the benefits have on overall inequality in old age. Again, poverty among the elderly usefully indicates the extent to which pension programs help those at the lowest end of the income distribution. Direct comparison of pension spending and poverty among the elderly can thus tell us much about national differences in the consequences of public pension programs.

Two cross-national studies of eight high-income nations done by the Organization of Economic Cooperation and Development (OECD) provide this information. One study (OECD 1992:34) compares the size of public and private pensions as a percentage of total income among households headed by people age 65 and over from 1978 to 1980. The first columns in Table 5.2 reproduce some of the figures from the study. Huge differences exist between nations in the size of public support for elderly households. For example, in elderly households in the United States, 40 percent of income comes from public pensions, 12 percent comes from private pensions, and the remainder comes from wages, savings, and other income sources. In contrast, elderly households in Sweden obtain 80 percent of their income from public pensions. As private pensions rarely exist in Sweden, the remainder of income comes from wages and savings.

Another OECD study (1988:47) compares the percentage of the elderly below poverty. According to the OECD statistics presented in the last column of Table 5.2, Sweden has poverty near zero, whereas the United States shows poverty of 20 percent among the elderly. (The figure for the United States exceeds the poverty rate reported by the U.S. government because the OECD uses a special measure that makes the cross-national comparisons meaningful.) The study considers those households with income less than half the median income to be in poverty. Like the United States, Canada and the United Kingdom have relatively high levels of poverty. Like Sweden, Norway and Australia show lower levels of poverty. Germany and Switzerland fall in between the extremes.

More important, nations with high public pension spending tend to have lower poverty levels among the elderly. Sweden and Norway, both with high public pension benefits, have the lowest poverty in old age. The United States, Canada, and the United Kingdom, nations with low public pension benefits, have relatively high levels of poverty. Australia and Switzerland, however, appear as exceptions to the relationship between reliance on public pensions and low poverty. Both spend little on public pension systems but appear to use the benefits to reduce poverty. Germany spends highly for public pensions but has poverty levels in the middle range of the distribution.

TABLE 5.2

National Differences in Pensions and Poverty among the Elderly

Nation	% Public Pensions	% Private Pensions	% Poverty Elderly
Sweden	80	0	0
Germany	71	12	9
Norway	58	6	5
United Kingdom	50	14	18
Australia	48	7	5
Canada	40	10	12
Switzerland	40	14	9
United States	40	12	20

Pension Regimes

How can we make sense of these national differences in pension spending, pension rights, and inequality? Together, the dimensions for comparing nations define three groups of nations with similar public pension systems. The grouping of nations into three policy regimes (or government strategies in relating to the private economy) helps simplify comparisons across nations and helps place the United States in comparative perspective. The classification comes from the work of Esping-Andersen (1990).

The first type of policy strategy or regime, labeled *social democratic* by Esping-Andersen, emphasizes social solidarity and equality in welfare benefits. The Scandinavian nations of Sweden, Norway, and Denmark best exemplify this type of regime. Policies generally make welfare benefits universally available to citizens, and pension policies make pension benefits universally available to older citizens. By providing similar benefits to all older citizens regardless of previous work history or financial contributions, social democratic pension systems highlight similarities across social and economic groups. Because those with few resources receive protection similar to workers with higher resources, all workers see themselves as "in the same boat."

By providing a base benefit to all older people as a right of citizenship, regardless of past work experience and earnings, universal benefits in social democratic regimes reduce some of the differences in wages that exist before old age. In absolute terms, they provide a minimum income for all older people that eliminates poverty in old age. In relative terms, equal benefits make for similarity in economic status between high- and low-income workers. High-income workers also supplement their basic flat-rate benefit with public and private occupational pensions that correspond closely to wages. Nevertheless, the payment of the same basic benefit to all older people encourages unity across diverse social groups.

A second type of regime, termed *conservative* by Esping-Andersen (1990), emphasizes programs that maintain existing status distinctions among workers. Conservative regimes such as in Germany, Italy, and France grant social rights to public support on the basis of occupational and industrial positions rather than on citizenship. Separate pension programs tend to develop for workers in different types of occupations or industries. For example, salaried and manual workers have their own programs, as do public and private sector workers. The motivation for public programs comes from the desire to protect workers and citizens, but to do so in a way that maintains the existing class differences rather than promotes equality and universalism.

The governments in conservative nations have played an active role in promoting welfare programs and pensions to gain the loyalty of workers. Ironically, conservative states developed welfare systems before many social democratic nations as a means to limit the threat of socialism to the traditional power of the government. Conservative nations also have a strong Catholic tradition that emphasizes social protection, but again through diversity rather than through similarity and equality. Because conservative states and Catholic ideology produce pension systems that favor the more privileged, high-salary employees, the middle class developed interests in continuing the existing system. Efforts by lower-status workers to replace the conservative model with more universal programs generally failed (Esping-Andersen 1990).

The third type of regime, termed *liberal* by Esping-Andersen, emphasizes the importance of market forces in determining social protection and pension benefits. Liberal means something different in comparing nations than it does in referring to political parties in the United States. In historical terms, liberals favored free markets and limited government in opposition to those favoring the traditional power of large landowners and the emerging power of labor unions. In comparing nations today, high-income, English-speaking nations—the United Kingdom, United States, Canada, Ireland, New Zealand, and Australia—typify liberal regimes.

In liberal regimes, pension benefits in old age stem primarily from market contributions and earnings during the work life. In fact, eligibility for public benefits requires many years of work and contribution, which penalizes those who leave the labor force because of family duties, unemployment, or health problems. Those who do not make sufficient contributions can receive more modest benefits from means-tested programs, but the benefits remain low to deter people from preferring welfare over work. Because public benefits in any form seldom provide enough income to generously support a person or couple, those with sufficient resources contribute to and receive private pensions. The need for workers to rely on private pensions further emphasizes the importance of the market relative to government intervention.

Because benefits differ substantially by work status and earnings in liberal regimes, old-age policies tend to reinforce market-based inequality. Poor people depend most on the less generous, means-tested benefits. Lower- and working-class people depend more on modest public contribution-based public benefits. Middle- and higher-income people depend less on public support of either type and more on private pension benefits and savings. In this way, the liberal nature of pension programs, such as those in the United States, helps maintain class, race, ethnic, and gender differences in old age.

In summary, the grouping of nations into three types of policy regimes demonstrates notable differences across nations in support of older people. As illustrated by concrete examples below, people will experience old age differently under the three types of pension systems.

IN THE UNITED STATES, a single person age 65 who does not qualify for Social Security benefits can obtain Supplemental Security Income and food stamps benefits worth about $5160 per year in 1991. This figure represents the minimum public benefit available to an older person. By comparison, someone working full-time for the low wage of $5 an hour will make $10,000 a year. In relative terms, the minimum benefit barely provides for subsistence living.

Now consider a single person age 65 in Denmark who also qualifies for only the minimum benefit. That person will get $6545 a year (translated into U.S. dollars) from an old-age pension available to all elderly citizens. Although the difference in minimum benefits in Denmark and the United States may seem small, the extra $1385 in Denmark will certainly help someone without other income sources.

In Germany, the same single person age 65 does worse than in either the United States or Denmark. Someone who does not qualify for a public pension receives social assistance benefits worth $4813—$347 less than in the United States. This amount, however low in absolute terms, appears even *lower relative to more advantaged retirees in Germany. A German retiree qualifying for the maximum benefit receives about five times as much as the minimum benefit. In the United States, maximum benefits are about two times as large as the minimum benefit; in Denmark, maximum benefits exceed minimum benefits only slightly (Palme 1990; Whiteford 1995).*

Even if programs in high-income nations treat average people similarly in old age, the poorest elderly will do better in some nations than in others. Similarly, the richest elderly will have fewer advantages in some nations than in others. Even without discussing all the details of a pension system in any particular nation, we can understand how the underlying philosophy of pension regimes influences individuals in later life.

Of course, as pension systems vary in benefits, they also vary in costs. According to 1991 figures, taxes per person reached $14,628 in Sweden and $12,219 in Denmark, compared to $8279 in Germany and $6550 in the United States (U.S. Bureau of the Census 1994:867). Relative to gross domestic product, taxes reach 53 percent in Sweden, 48 percent in Denmark, 39 percent in Germany, and 30 percent in the United States. At least until recently, citizens in social democratic and conservative regimes have shown themselves quite willing to shoulder the costs of generous social security programs. Citizens in liberal regimes such as the United States and the United Kingdom also desire generous social protection but react more negatively to the high taxes needed to support them.

In the future, however, social democratic and conservative regimes may find it difficult to maintain current government spending. With low unemployment and a relatively small aged population, generous benefits and high taxes created few problems for nations such as Sweden or Germany. In the past few years, growing unemployment and an aging population have strained the budgets of many European nations. They now face painful cuts in benefits, as in Sweden, or further increases in taxes, as in Germany. During this period of global competition among national economies, social democratic and conservative regimes will have to debate how far to move away from universalism and how close to move toward models of liberal regimes.

Aging and Pension Support in Japan

Although a high-income nation with a democratic political system, low fertility and mortality rates, and an advanced industrial economy, Japan differs from European nations in the treatment of its elderly. On one hand, government support for the elderly has remained low relative to European nations. On the other hand, a tradition of respect for elders in Japan provides high levels of family support for older people. Because of the special nature of public and private support, scholars have devoted much effort to answering the question, "Is aging better in Japan?"

Those who answer "no" to this question make several points. First, comprehensive public policies for the elderly do not compare in generosity or universality to those in Europe. In Esping-Andersen's scheme, Japan fits the conservative model. The figures on public pension spending in Figure 5.2 list Japan near the bottom rank among the high-income nations. In addition, public pension benefits differ greatly for low- and high-income workers. According to Table 5.1, the maximum public retirement replacement rate is more than 7 times greater than the minimum rate. Besides public pension programs, Japan does not offer other comprehensive social services for the elderly or provide for retirement housing and nursing home care (Palmore 1993).

Second, despite efforts by the Japanese government to improve their public programs for the elderly, population changes are occurring too quickly for policies to have much of an effect. Although Japan has a relatively small aged population (12 percent compared to 18 percent in Sweden), it also has the fastest rate of growth of the aged population in the world. Because fertility has fallen quickly in Japan since World War II, and because Japan has the longest life expectancy in the world, the size of the elderly population relative to the younger population has grown quickly. The suddenness of the aging of the population will make for a difficult adjustment in support of the elderly in Japan.

Third, the recent modernization in the Japanese economy has reduced the traditional respect and favorable treatment accorded older people. The sudden shift to an industrialized economy focused on trade with the West has left young people raised during this period of modernization resentful of the demands made by older generations for obedience and care. At the same time, older people raised during the early part of the century feel bitter that they do not get the respect that their parents did many decades ago. Lacking generous public support, older people must depend on their family at a time when tensions across generations seem to be increasing (Ogawa and Retherford 1997). As illustrated by the story below, the Japanese may express ritual respect for the elderly, but their actual feelings are more negative (Koyano 1989).

SIXTY-NINE-YEAR-OLD Mrs. Watari lives "in a tiny, two-room house, consisting of one six tatami-mat room, a small kitchen, a bathroom, and a toilet. It is separated by a high metal fence from a large modern, attractive home in a residential area of Setagayaku. It is located on what was once the garden of the big house. Flowers and shrubs no longer grow there. . . . Mrs. Watari has been living in this humble house for two years. Before that, she lived in the big house next door with her son, daughter-in-law, and grandson. She was shocked when her son announced that his wife requested that she move from the home that she and her son have occupied for many years before his marriage six years ago" (Freed 1992:91).

Now, her son comes to visit only once a week. Although hurt and lonesome, Mrs. Watari understands that "these days many daughters do not want old parents, especially a mother-in-law, around" (Freed 1992:96).

Those who answer "yes" to the question "Is aging better in Japan?" highlight the strong family ties between older people and their children. Although Japan lacks the kind of formal, bureaucratic sources of support common in the West, the elderly do not need that kind of support because they are so strongly integrated into the family and workforce. Indeed, the elderly receive special respect that is rare, if not completely absent, in Western nations.

IT MAKES SENSE THAT THE HEROES and heroines in an older society are not the likes of youthful rock stars or 20-something movie actors, and indeed, Japan may be a step ahead of other countries by hailing geriatric celebrities. Because of their old age, Gin-San and Kin-san, a pair of 104-year old twins, have become celebrities in Japan. "When someone asked them what they were doing with the money from all their public appearances, Gin-san smiled and explained, 'We're saving it for our old age'" (Kristof 1996:4-1). In their attitude toward the future, Gin-san and Kin-san typify more general attitudes toward time in Japan. In Robert Smith's (1961) description,

> *The older adult is not, then, a prisoner of time, nor does he feel that time is running out for him. He makes no effort to appear younger than he is. The minutes, hours, and days simply pass filled up with a variety of activities, which are performed as the need to do them arises. Time does not drag and it does not threaten; it is to be used but it does not stretch emptily before the older person. (p. 99)*

In terms of the family, living arrangements of the elderly in Japan reveal high levels of private support. In 1991, 77 percent of women ages 75 and over shared housing with their adult children; the same figure for the United States is only 22 percent (Yashiro 1997:90). Although household sharing reached even higher levels several decades ago and has fallen since then, support by younger family members of their older parents remains strong compared to Western nations. Conversely, older parents also help younger family members by caring for young children and sharing the high costs of housing (Morgan and Hirosima 1983). Given this type of informal family support across generations, older people in Japan require less formal government support. In terms of work, the continued employment of many people in Japan during old age also reduces the need for a generous public pension program. In Japan, where many firms hire employees under an agreement of lifetime employment, retirement typically takes the form of reduced hours and less responsibility on the job rather than complete withdrawal from the labor force. Thus, older people in Japan receive more wage income than do older people in the United States (Yashiro 1997).

In terms of respect, the elderly in Japan remain objects of honor. Annual celebration of the Respect for Elders day has no equivalent in Western nations. Elders receive priority in seating, serving, bathing, and going through doors; they are addressed by special names to indicate the honor they deserve; and younger people bow longer and lower to the elderly than to others (Palmore and Maeda 1985). Although seemingly of minor importance by themselves, these daily actions of respect reflect widespread support for the elderly. As Kinoshita and Kiefer (1993) say,

> Japanese culture appears to encourage old people to be socially responsible and to venerate the aged themselves. . . . Japan is traditionally a family-centered society in which the elderly members appear to be better socially integrated than their counterparts in the West. (p. 5)

Overall, a reasonable conclusion to these debates would say that aging in Japan differs from the West—better in some ways and worse in others. The judgment one makes about the differences depends on values and beliefs. For some, the high levels of integration of the elderly into the family, work, and cultural life of Japan more than make up for weak government programs; others may think the opposite (Palmore 1993).

Sources of National Divergence

To understand why nations have adopted quite different types of pension programs and represent quite different pension regimes, it helps to consider the logic behind competing philosophies of the welfare state. National differences in pension policy programs (and the welfare state more generally) reflect two basic and fundamentally contradictory principles (Myles 1984). One principle based on the growth of capitalist economies reflects the logic of the free market. From this perspective, pensions represent wages set aside for old age in place of current payment and should reflect wage differences during the work life of pensioners. The government merely administers the transfer of current wages into later pensions.

The other principle stems from the presence of political democracy in capitalist economies. Democracy emphasizes equality and citizenship rights rather than inequality in wages and salaries. By giving the vote to all adult citizens, democracy in ideal terms treats individuals as equal in political rights despite their different economic resources. Democratic pressures for equality would tend to favor universal programs for pensions and other social needs rather than programs based on economic contributions. The state would actively aid in the redistribution of economic resources. In this sense, political processes differ fundamentally from economic processes in determining the basis for pension receipt in old age.

Capitalist democracies reveal the presence of—and tension between—both principles in their pension laws (Myles 1984). Nations such as Germany and the United States emphasize market-based pension programs under the influence of the free-market principle, but they also offer programs for minimum benefits based on the democratic principle. Other nations, such as Denmark, Sweden, and the United Kingdom, emphasize universal, flat-rate benefit programs consistent with the democratic principle, but they also offer earnings-related programs for higher-income workers based on the free-market principle.

Debates over current public policies stem in large part from the tensions between these principles. Opinions about the level of taxes, the generosity of pension benefits, and the degree of equality in benefits reflect larger perspectives over the relative roles that democracy and the private market should play in social and economic life. To understand the sources of national divergence, then, we need to examine the social groups that tend to favor each of the competing principles. We also need to examine differences across nations in the power of these social groups. Historically, social classes defined the divisions most relevant to conflict over social welfare programs.

Class Interests

Groups with the most economic resources and power—owners, managers, middle classes—tend to prefer allowing the private market rather than democratic processes to determine economic standing. By shifting economic power away from the private sector to the state sector, public pensions reduce the resources of otherwise privileged classes (Shalev 1983). Members of the advantaged classes therefore emphasize the importance of economic freedom—that is, freedom from interference by the government—in making contracts, trading, and bargaining in the marketplace (Myles 1984). The higher the level of taxes, and the greater the public benefits available to workers outside the labor market, the less the market-based freedom of individuals and organizations. Owners of private wealth prefer retirement systems based on private pensions, low taxes, and close ties to the free market.

In contrast, workers with fewer economic resources can compete better in democratic political processes because of their relatively large numbers and potential voting power (Korpi 1983). Workers tend to emphasize the importance of political freedom—equal participation in government decisions—in determining economic standing (Myles 1984). They prefer retirement systems based on public rather than private pensions, need rather than contributions, and equality rather than inequality in benefits. Government programs should therefore grow at the expense of private programs, and private programs should face more government regulation.

Debate over pension programs involves democratic conflict between classes. Some describe the conflict as a new form of class conflict: Where classes once battled primarily in the form of wage negotiations, strikes, and lockouts, they now battle over social policy in legislatures (Piven and Cloward 1982). The conflict has moved from the factory to the government; one side wants to extend democratic processes to the private sector, and the other side wants to maintain a more distinct separation of politics and the economy.

What determines the relative balance of the economic power of owners and managers to the democratic power of workers? One answer focuses on the size and organization of workers in the form of labor unions. Despite having similarly sized working classes, nations differ in the percentage of the labor force belonging to labor unions (Western 1993). Equally important, nations differ in the degree to which workers have organized themselves into centralized unions that unite members from diverse occupations, industries, and regions. Large and powerful union organizations can, in turn, mobilize workers in elections to support parties that will attempt to implement universal programs of social protection. Nations with weak, small, and decentralized unions face problems in recruiting new members, acting cooperatively, and mobilizing political support. Without strong unions, workers in some nations have less political power relative to employers and less success in electing parties that support their interests.

Esping-Andersen (1990) relates differences across pension regimes directly to the power of labor unions and leftist political parties supported by unions. Social democratic regimes with generous, universal, and egalitarian pension programs emerged in nations with strong labor movements and popular leftist political parties. Liberal regimes with relatively small, market-based public pension programs emerged in nations with divided labor movements and strong rightist parties supported by business and the middle classes. Conservative regimes with generous but inegalitarian pension programs emerged in nations with religious-based unions and political parties (Huber et al. 1993); labor unions in these nations had more power than labor unions in liberal nations, but less than in social democratic nations.

Classes in the United States

How do these class-based arguments apply to the historical experiences of the United States? Like other nations, businesses in the United States have historically opposed public pension programs. Large businesses preferred private negotiation with workers, and smaller businesses wanted to avoid altogether the cost of social security provisions (Quadagno 1984). Workers and unions, in contrast, have favored such programs. Debates over pension policy have, in the past, reflected (and still do today) these class-based viewpoints.

Unlike most European nations, however, a divided labor movement in the United States could not agree on a common approach to public programs. Differences in the positions and interests of craft, semiskilled, unskilled, and nonmanual workers prevented the united support of workers for universal pension programs found in other nations. Similarly, regional, ethnic, and racial divisions split interests in ways that further inhibited unity among the working class. Different interests between white and black workers, northern and southern workers, and native-born and immigrant workers contributed to a weak union movement and a pension program based on market rather than democratic principles.

The particular experience of industrial development in the United States also contributed to a weak labor movement and slowed the emergence of a unified public pension program. Along with Great Britain, the United States experienced early industrial development. The unprecedented changes brought about by early industrialization made central planning and organization difficult for business owners, the government, and advocates of workers. Other nations experiencing later industrial development knew more of what to expect. They could more easily specialize in certain types of products and plan for more orderly industrial expansion. As a result, workers proved much harder to organize into centralized unions in the United States than in many European nations (Stephens 1986). As shown in Figure 5.3, huge differences remain to this day in union membership—from under 15 percent in the United States to more than 90 percent in Sweden (Western 1993).

In addition, the large size of the United States made union organization difficult. In smaller countries with smaller domestic markets for sale of industrial products, businesses become more concentrated with a fewer number of firms (Katzenstein 1985; Stephens 1986). The concentration of work in a smaller number of firms made a unified union movement possible. In the geographically huge and ethnically diverse United States, industries, firms, or unions could not concentrate to the same extent as many smaller European nations.

Along with a divided labor movement, the lack of a social democratic political party closely associated with the labor movement limited working-class power in the United States. Constitutional rules for elections have promoted two dominant parties, each of which represents diverse interests. The Democratic party has historically combined the interests of workers, who desired generous public spending, with those of farmers and southerners, who did not. The lack of a separate labor or social democratic party, such as emerged in most European nations, to advocate the interests of workers blocked the development of a universal and generous pension system in the United States.

Role of the Middle Class

A criticism of these arguments also focuses on the role of class in the emergence of welfare state programs, but it attributes more importance to the role of the middle class than to the working class. The working-class strength hypothesis assumes that blue-collar workers face the greatest risk of loss of work and income in old age, and therefore have the most to gain from a generous pension program. Yet Peter Baldwin (1990) rejects these arguments by asserting that the working class historically has not always been in the most vulnerable economic position. Accordingly,

FIGURE 5.3

Union Membership

it has not always been the strongest advocate of a universal program. His study of class resources and political positions in Europe finds that social security programs emerged from the interests among many different groups rather than from working-class pressure for expanded benefits against middle-class resistance.

According to Baldwin, universal pensions in the Scandinavian nations emerged from the demands of the middle classes rather than labor. The urban middle class opposed programs that targeted benefits to workers and excluded other groups, and it desired universal programs that spread benefits initially available only to urban workers. Center parties representing agricultural workers also played a crucial role in passage of pension programs that covered all workers. Changes in technology and low crop prices meant that peasants, small landowners, and agricultural laborers in Scandinavia faced greater economic problems than did urban workers.

In Britain, similar processes led to the development of universal programs several decades later. Economic changes during the post–World

War II period threatened the status of independent employers and small businesses. The heightened economic risks of the middle classes increased their stake in a broad welfare program. Combined with their political power, the risks faced by the middle classes made it possible to pass universal legislation. Parties of the right and center again participated actively in welfare reform in Britain.

In Germany and France, universal welfare programs failed to gain the support of middle-class groups. Because workers in Germany and France stayed most vulnerable to economic risks of loss of income, the middle classes had little interest in or need for welfare benefits—they could continue to rely on private, market-based support. Political pressure from workers most in need could not overcome opposition of the middle classes. Without some sort of alliance, workers and leftist parties rarely had the power to implement generous and universal welfare programs.

Applying Baldwin's arguments to the United States would highlight the reliance of middle-class workers, and even high-status, working-class members, on private pension systems. Little incentive existed for them to participate in a universal public system. As a result, public pension programs emerged to supplement private pensions and savings rather than to replace existing programs. The lack of middle-class interest in a generous pension program in the United States, along with a weak working class, contributed to the low spending levels and late development of Social Security.

State Structure

Factors other than class power contribute to national differences in public pensions. The structure of the state or government has received much attention from scholars in recent years (Evans, Reuschemeyer, and Skocpol 1985; Skocpol 1995). For example, even if a majority of voters in the United States desired more generous and universal programs, the nature of the federal government in the United States has made passage of the necessary legislation difficult. State governments play a more important governing role in the United States than in most high-income nations. The development of different and separate programs in individual states may have slowed the emergence of a national program.

Similarly, the system of checks and balances in the United States has made passage of comprehensive old-age programs difficult. Representatives from a small number of states or certain types of special interests opposed to a national pension program could block legislation given the numerous checks and balances in the American political system. The diffusion of power across states, courts, executive agencies, and legislatures in the complex federal system of government gave veto power to minority interests who could block legislation for a national pension program (Huber et al. 1993).

Another characteristic of government in the United States in the early 20th century—the lack of a professional civil service bureaucracy to administer pension systems—may have slowed passage of national legislation (Orloff and Skocpol 1984). In Britain, a professional national welfare bureaucracy made distribution of pension benefits across the nation relatively easy. In the United States at the turn of the century, supporters of victorious political candidates rather than the best qualified people filled civil servant positions. Fearing corruption of local governments and national agencies, many voters opposed a national pension system that would make misuse of pension funds that much easier.

Theda Skocpol (1992) emphasizes that by the turn of the century in the United States, substantial portions of elderly and disabled veterans of the Civil War received pensions from the military. Consistent with the state structure argument, this type of program suited the political environment in the United States. Veterans could rely on their local congressional representative in Washington, D.C., rather than a central and professional bureaucracy to help them gain benefits. However, the system also promoted fraud. Skocpol (1992) reports a story originally published in a magazine in 1910:

A MAN NAMED WILLIAM NEWBY . . . was killed at Shiloh, April 6, 1862, and buried on the battle-field by his comrades. . . . His widow moved from Illinois to Texas and his family had grown up and scattered by the year 1891, when a stranger walked into the streets of the Texan town and announced himself as William Newby. His story was that a wound on the head had made him insane, that he had wandered, and had only lately regained memory of his identity. The Widow Newby was sent for, and after a little talk declared that this was her missing husband. Now Mrs. Newby had for thirty years been pensioned as a veteran's widow. The restored "Newby" immediately applied for a pension. His stake was a large one, his claim [with arrears] being $15,000. (p. 146)

Their suspicions aroused by abuse of the Civil War pension system, Congress was unwilling to pass a more comprehensive public pension system until the Great Depression of the 1930s.

A Feminist Critique

Another perspective on the nature of pension systems comes from those concentrating on the treatment of women. Feminist critics note that most theories and measures of pension programs concentrate on the average manufacturing worker—a man in nearly all countries. When they include women explicitly, the measures treat them as nonworking partners in elderly couples who share benefits earned by males. The only study calculating replacement rates for women finds little, if any, relationship to benefits for men (Tracy and Ward 1986).

The feminist critique not only considers measurement issues, but it also highlights the failure of pension systems to address the particular problems of women in old age (Orloff 1993). As discussed in the previous chapter, women do not participate in the labor force to the same degree as do men, and they do not make the same contributions to public and private pension funds. Even in Scandinavia, work-based benefits that supplement universal benefits favor full-time male workers over part-time and unpaid female workers. Until men and women share domestic duties equally—not a change yet realized in any high-income nation—motherhood and marriage result in lower pension benefits under all types of existing pension systems.

Orloff (1993) suggests that public pension programs need to take a more active role in countering male advantages by addressing women's special problems directly. Policies could do this by shifting the burden of domestic work, such as for child care, to public agencies. They could also provide pension benefits to homemakers independent of those for the male breadwinner. Finally, they could do more to guarantee women access to jobs with high pay and pension coverage, and reduce the importance of seniority requirements. All of these changes would require substantial revisions of all types of pension systems.

Lewis (1992) compares some of the European nations on the extent to which their welfare systems value unpaid work done by women. She identifies Britain and Ireland as strong male breadwinner states because their policies do not encourage female work and make wives and mothers dependent on male wages and pension benefits. Policies do little to ease the entrance of women into the labor force, requiring that they compete with men for jobs and salaries without special compensation for their child and home care duties. As a result, inequality emerges in husbands' and wives' pension contributions and benefits in old age.

Lewis identifies France as a modified male breadwinner state because women participate more fully in the labor force than in Britain or Ireland, but nevertheless remain fully responsible for mothering duties. Although women depend less on male breadwinners than in some nations, they still face penalties from home duties. Finally, Lewis identifies Sweden as a weak male breadwinner state because policies provide for child care, maternity benefits, and parental leave for working women. Although far from complete, such policies increase female labor force participation beyond levels in most other nations and help make women financially independent from spouses during old age.

The treatment of women by Social Security in the United States most resembles the treatment in Britain. Women can receive benefits based on their own earnings or, more often, on those of their husbands. As a result, working women may receive benefits no larger than nonworking women. Also under present rules, a spouse loses pension benefits earned by the other spouse if they divorce before 10 years of marriage. Several proposals in recent years advocate giving pension credit for child care years, including Social Security benefits in property settlements, and sharing combined earnings equally (Rejda 1994). However, such proposals have made little progress given problems of deficit spending.

Conclusion

Comparisons of public pension systems among the high-income nations show wide diversity. At one time, scholars expected that as nations reached similarly high levels of economic development, they would produce similar systems of public support for retired people. Instead, trends over time have, if anything, increased pension program differences across the high-income nations. Despite economic and technological pressures toward similarity, national differences in the political composition of governments, the strength of the working and middle classes, and the structure of the state produce differences in public policy. In the area of pensions, nations differ in the levels of spending, the emphasis on citizen entitlement, and the impact of programs on inequality and poverty.

The national comparisons offered in this chapter provide a broader perspective on the special nature of pension programs in the United States. Compared to other high-income nations, the United States relies more strongly on private pensions than public pensions: Its public pension programs spend and tax less as a percentage of GDP and less per older person than nearly all high-income nations. Pension programs in the United States also do less to reduce market inequality in old age than do other nations; instead, they favor those who did best during the work years. Such a system proves consistent with values of individualism and distrust of government authority, but it stems more directly from a weak union movement, a divided leftist party, and a decentralized state structure.

Regardless of the causes, the special nature of pension programs in the United States emphasizes the importance of political decisions relative to forces of poor health and biological changes in old age. The study of other nations reveals the alternative approaches that American public policy for the elderly might have employed instead. Where Scandinavian nations rely on universal public benefits, high taxes, and a huge role for the government in the daily lives of their citizens, Japan relies more on informal private support of the elderly. Such differences in national policy strongly affect the nature of old age.

6

Inequality across Age Groups and Generations

STRUGGLING TO PAY HIS WAY through college, Dan works evenings parking cars at an exclusive and expensive country club near his college in Florida. Winter is the busiest time of the year because many retired members have come south to enjoy the warm weather. As he parks the Cadillac of another obviously wealthy retired couple, Dan begins to think about Social Security. To him, it seems like taking from the young and poor to help the old and well off. He works for $5.50 an hour and tips but pays about 40 cents of each hour's wage for Social Security. His employer pays another 40 cents—a total of about 15 percent of his earnings. That doesn't sound like much, but month after month, it begins to add up. Over the year, he and his boss contribute nearly a thousand dollars. If he could keep the money he now pays for Social Security taxes and receive as pay the contributions his employer makes to Social Security for him, it would make a huge difference in his life. He could better afford the expensive tuition and room and board in college, and he could spend more time studying rather than working. Instead, that desperately needed $1000 might go to the wealthy older couple whose car he just parked. It does not seem fair that, with his low income, the government takes his money to give to someone else better off than he is.

MICHELLE LOOKS AT SOCIAL SECURITY differently. Her parents help her with the costs of college so that she will not have to work so much. However, it can be a strain on her parents. The costs of $20,000 a year seem difficult for everyone. Still, it could have been worse. Her widowed grandmother recently was diagnosed with cancer and had to endure expensive and painful chemotherapy. Fortunately for her and her parents, Medicare covered nearly all the costs. Because her grandmother could never have paid for the treatment, the bill would have fallen on her parents. And with expensive medical bills, her parents would not have been able to help her in college. Michelle realizes that the same logic holds for Social Security. Because government *retirement benefits go to her grandmother, it spares her parents from having to provide the support themselves. Indirectly, then, Michelle benefits from Social Security. What helps one generation also helps the others.*

Individual aging varies across social classes, races, ethnic groups, and genders, and it varies across nations with different class structures, political systems, and public pension programs. Still one other source of variation in aging—membership in different generations—has become particularly relevant to political debates today. Although "generation" has many meanings, it refers here to people born during the same historical period who, despite many individual differences, accumulate a common set of experiences peculiar to them (Thomson 1993:217). In terms of aging, the historical timing of a generation's entrance into old age affects the kinds of experiences its members can expect.

In general, generations entering old age in recent decades experienced a different and generally more supportive environment than did previous generations. The decline in poverty among the elderly since the 1970s has benefited people who were born after the turn of the century and reached old age during a time of rising government support. Those born before 1900, who reached old age before the 1970s, experienced higher rates of poverty by virtue of when their generation entered old age.

In addition, the current generation of older people on average seems better off now than do younger generations. If the generational disadvantage of young people lasts, they will also experience a less supportive environment during old age than the current elderly enjoy. Generational differences in government support for the elderly thus raise issues of fairness that involve both younger and older generations. As illustrated by the stories of Dan and Michelle, issues of fairness surface in debates over current and future Social Security policies in the United States.

This chapter views current differences between younger people and older people as an aspect of generational change. Just as recent social, economic, and political trends have changed inequality *within* the aged population, they have also changed inequality *across* age groups and generations. The next sections consider the consequences of population aging for generational differences and then compare those consequences in the United States today with those in earlier historical periods and other nations. Throughout, the discussion concentrates on the well-being of the elderly and children—the youngest and oldest generations alive today.

Consequences of Population Aging

In discussing policy successes in support for older people in the United States, Chapter 1 compared trends in poverty among the elderly relative to children. Although important differences exist within age groups, older people as a group have done better than children as a group. Whereas families with children experienced increasing rates of poverty from the late 1970s to the 1990s, poverty among the elderly declined dramatically. Perhaps for the first time in the history of the United States, the risks of poverty for children have come to exceed those for the elderly.

Along with economic fortunes, the political fortunes of the elderly relative to children seem to have improved. As also discussed in earlier chapters, government spending for social assistance and job programs, typically directed to young parents with children, fell during the 1980s in terms of real dollars and as a proportion of the total government budget. At the same time that spending for children declined, spending for pensions and health care for the elderly grew remarkably. If not the dominant cause of the reversal in the economic standing of children and the elderly, public spending nevertheless corresponds closely to trends in age inequality.

Rather than isolated phenomena, the economic and political trends among children and the elderly reflect broader patterns of change. Along with other problems, children and young people have experienced higher rates of mortality from homicide and suicide; poorer school performance; and increased problems from delinquency, drug and alcohol use; and child abuse. In contrast, the elderly as a group have experienced lower rates of mortality, fewer years of work obligations, and a newly found sense of pride. In many ways, then, recent trends exhibit divergent trajectories of the well-being of children and the elderly.

Preston (1984) emphasizes the importance of demographic forces for these changes in the well-being of America's two dependent age groups. The size of the child and youth population has declined as a proportion of the total population in recent decades because of declining fertility. The size of the aged population has risen as a proportion of the total population because of declining fertility and declining mortality at the older ages. Many would expect that a declining population of children would improve their well-being for the simple reason that a smaller number of children would have to share the resources devoted to them by families and the government. Also, a growing aged population would mean greater deprivation for older people, because a larger number of people have to share the available resources.

Instead, a large aged population, composed mostly of middle-class, politically active retirees, has increased its political influence. A declining child population, many of whom are from single-parent, disadvantaged families, has reduced the political influence of families with children. Greater political power has in turn increased the public benefits available to the elderly, and weaker political power has reduced the public benefits available to families with children. Efforts to alleviate the historic financial plight of older people have had success: The current elderly comprise both the largest and richest generation of older people in American history.

If the size of age groups translates into political power, the trends in the status of children and the elderly will continue to diverge. People age 65 and over made up 12.6 percent of the population in 1990, and according to projections, they will increase slowly in the next 20 years to 13.9 percent in 2010 (U.S. Bureau of the Census 1994). However, 20 years later, in 2030, the projections predict that the elderly will make up 21.8 percent of the population—almost doubling in 40 to 50 years.

To put this number in perspective, recall from the previous chapter that Sweden, the nation with the oldest population in the world today, has 17 percent elderly. By 2030, the United States will substantially exceed this figure. Similar comparisons within the United States also demonstrate the immensity of the change in age structure. Figure 6.1 charts the percentage of elderly in the 15 oldest and 15 youngest states in 1993. The state with the oldest population in the country, Florida, currently has almost 19 percent elderly. In several decades, the nation as a whole will exceed that percentage (Uhlenberg 1992). Although all other states have relatively small aged populations now, they will become more like Florida in decades to come.

The trends in population aging, public spending, and poverty have generated a good deal of controversy. One debate has developed in terms of *generational inequity:* Do the elderly get more and children get less than they deserve and need? On one side of the debate, some claim that rising public support of older people has harmed the young. Given limited funds for public social welfare, expanding benefits for the elderly have left fewer funds for children. On the other side of the debate, critics of these claims believe that the elderly and children do not compete for the same income and public benefits. Because they both depend on government support, children and the elderly find themselves linked more as allies than competitors. Framing the debate as if the elderly benefit at the expense of children only creates an artificial wedge between generations

FIGURE 6.1

State Differences in Aged Population

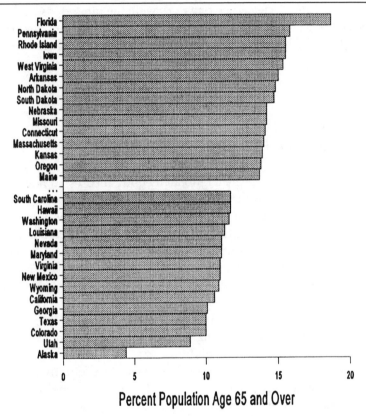

Percent Population Age 65 and Over

and offers an excuse to cut benefits for the elderly rather than raise them for children.

Note that the debate shifts the issue from *inequality or equality* between age groups to *inequity or equity* between age groups. Inequality refers to differences in resources available to groups; inequity refers to the gap between what a group receives and what a group deserves. Without claiming that children and the elderly should receive equal or identical forms of support, generational inequity means that children receive less than they deserve, and the elderly receive more than they deserve. The issue becomes one of fairness and deservingness.

To some degree, comparing children and the elderly ignores differences within age groups and oversimplifies the nature of inequality. Still, the debate over generational inequity raises issues especially relevant to young people by highlighting the connections that exist across age groups. Do the statuses of young and old correlate inversely so that, given limited resources, when one does well, the other does poorly? Or do the statuses correlate directly so that lack of support for one threatens support for the other, and high resources for one contributes resources for the other?

The Nature and Sources of Generational Inequity

Much of the concern over generational inequity focuses on how current government spending on the elderly costs young people today and will cost future generations of young people. Because spending for the elderly represents a substantial portion of the federal budget, improving benefits for children without a tax increase (that would fall largely on families with children) must come in part from current benefits for the elderly. Whereas military spending, government administration, social assistance, and other parts of the budget have already faced cuts, spending directed to the elderly has continued to grow steadily. The remaining alternative would require shifting public expenditures that currently go to the elderly to programs for children.

Lester Thurow (1996a) has stated these concerns bluntly in a recent newspaper article: "Already the needs and demands of the elderly have shaken the social welfare state, causing it for all practical purposes to go broke" (p. 46). He says that today, half of the federal budget goes to the elderly. "By 2003 expenditures on the elderly, plus interest payments will take 75 percent, and by 2013 they will take 100 percent, if current laws remain unchanged" (p. 46). Thurow goes on to note that these spending demands for the elderly have squeezed spending on other programs, including those for children.

A Reversal of Generational Support

Current high levels of public spending for the elderly reflect generational differences. Older people today belong to the generations born before World War II. They gained from the economic boom of the 1950s and from expanded spending on Social Security and Medicare since the 1970s. Children, youth, and middle-age people today, those belonging to generations born after World War II, have not enjoyed the same financial prosperity.

According to those concerned with generational inequity, the costs to young people of current patterns of government spending will only get worse. Younger generations now pay more in taxes for Social Security and Medicare than did previous generations. In the future, they will have to pay even higher taxes during adulthood and middle age to pay interest on accumulated government debt and to support elderly baby boomers. Current deficit spending requires borrowing that future generations must later repay in the form of higher taxes (Longman 1987). Critics sometimes use the term "mortgaging the future of our children" to emphasize the cost to future generations of current government borrowing. The difficulties of paying off the debt combined with the expense of supporting an ever-growing population of retirees make the economic future of younger generations look bleak.

High spending for the elderly may have another negative consequence for the future of today's children and for children not yet born. Government spending on children and their families for health care, nutrition, and education represents an investment in the future, as well as a means to raise productivity of future workers and maximize future economic growth. New generations—indeed, citizens of all ages—will enjoy the benefits of current investments in decades to come. In contrast, government spending for consumption brings short-term, but not long-term, benefits. Most spending for the elderly goes to consumption rather than to investment (Preston 1984). The elderly deserve support for their previous work, but in terms of wise investment, spending on children will pay greater dividends in the future.

An economist, Laurence Kotlikoff (1992), measures the implications of current government spending patterns for future generations with a procedure he terms "generational accounting." He estimates how much different generations can expect to pay over their lives in taxes and how much they can expect to receive in benefits. Although calculations such as these make assumptions about the future that may not hold, they nevertheless forecast a disconcerting picture of the costs of current public spending patterns. According to Kotlikoff, people age 25 in 1989 will pay $193,000 more in taxes than they will receive in government benefits over their lifetime. In contrast, people age 75 in 1989 will receive $42,000 more in government benefits than they paid in taxes.

It appears that today's elderly have received an excellent deal. Current retirees receive benefits well exceeding all their contributions to Social Security plus interest. They have paid less and consumed more, whereas younger people will pay more and consume less. In Kotlikoff's (1992) words, "U.S. generational policy is seriously out of balance" (p. xiv). Although generational inequity in the past reflected the disadvantaged status of the elderly relative to the nonaged, generational inequity today highlights the advantaged status of older people relative to other age groups, particularly children.

The high support of the elderly and the low support for children and future generations represent an enormous change in the nature of generational relations. Thomson (1993) argues that in the past, people accepted low income during old age as a necessary consequence of social needs to invest in young people. In the past several decades, however, rising benefits and income for the elderly, and declining benefits and income for children and young families, shifts the nature of support across generations. Now, younger adults with children pay taxes to support the elderly, often at the expense of their own financial well-being. In Thomson's view, this generational favoritism has reversed historical patterns of exchange.

Some members of the baby-boom generation react negatively to this reversal of support and attribute the problem in part to older generations now benefiting from current spending patterns. Now age 50, Joe Klein, a columnist for *Newsweek* magazine, was born in 1946—the very start of the post-World War II baby boom. Consistent with the beliefs of those concerned about generational inequity, Klein reacts negatively to organizations that represent the narrow interests of the elderly. In his *Newsweek* column, he writes:

> I've just received an interesting piece of mail: an invitation to join the American Association of Retired People. Yikes. All right. We all get old. Even baby boomers. But being a classic self-absorbed, quasi-messianic member of my generation, I cannot let the occasion pass without deep reflection. Actually, some deep reflection may be called for here. As our demographically grotesque horde drifts toward decrepitude, a significant political decision looms. Do we really want to support a group that is arguably the most powerful lobby in Washington and has become, over time, a narrow, encrusted and slightly cheesy bastion of anachronistic liberalism? . . . As for me, I won't join AARP until I'm convinced it's as concerned about my children's well being as it is about mine. (Klein 1995:27)

One also hears these sorts of claims about unfairness from members of the so-called Generation X, born during the 1960s and 1970s. They have already experienced the growth of poverty and rising divorce while children, limited economic opportunities while young adults, and high taxes while working adults. Some members of this generation criticize older generations for leaving them a bleak economic future and attribute the pessimism and cynicism of young people to the problems they face (Strauss and Howe 1991).

DOUGLAS COUPLAND DID NOT INVENT the term "Generation X," but he used it as the title of a novel that portrays the experiences of members of the post-baby-boom generation. A tale of bitterness and despair, the novel has became a cult classic and a publishing success (Rushkoff 1994). The attitude of Coupland's characters about older generations particularly reflects this bitterness and despair. One 20-something character expresses his feelings to someone older and wealthier: "Do you really think we enjoy hearing about your brand new million-dollar home when we can barely afford to eat Kraft dinner sandwiches in our own grimy little shoe boxes and we're pushing thirty? A home you won in a genetic lottery, I might add, sheerly by dint of your having been born at the right time in history. . . . I have to endure pinheads like you . . . always grabbing the best piece of cake first and then putting a barbed-wire fence around the rest" (Coupland 1991:21).

Although perhaps not typical of young people today, the attitudes expressed by the character and the novel uncover tensions across generations.

The Need for Policy Changes

Those concerned with generational inequity conclude that policymakers need to direct more resources away from current consumption and toward investment in the future. The high level of spending for the elderly burdens future citizens rather than invests in them. Although programs for the elderly do not represent the only target for reduced spending, the high costs of Social Security and Medicare make them necessary parts of any effort to control the government deficit.

One possible change in policy would involve making Social Security more like a social assistance program than a social insurance program. Providing fewer benefits to affluent older people and concentrating payments to those most in need would lower the overall costs of the program. An accompanying change would allow workers to invest some of the contributions they now make to Social Security in stock funds for their own use during retirement. Both changes would reduce the dependence of many future retirees on public pension benefits.

The Cato Institute, a conservative think-tank in Washington, D.C., that advocates making Social Security private, has created a web site (http://www.socialsecurity.org) to illustrate how private retirement systems might work. The web site allows one to calculate the benefits people of various ages and incomes would receive if they invested their Social Security contributions in the stock and bond market. Figure 6.2 charts the yearly income that people born in 1948 with salaries of $20,000 and $60,000 could expect from Social Security if they retire at age 66. Low-salary people would get about $9720 a year from Social Security and about $54,500 from investing the same contributions in a stock fund with a 10 percent return. Less risky bond and mixed bond/stock funds provide less than the stock fund, but still substantially more than Social Security. The advantages of bond and stock funds appear even greater for those with salaries of $60,000. These figures look attractive to those worried about supporting themselves in old age.

Other changes in social policy for the elderly need to address growth in spending for Medicare. Public expenditures for health care in general and for health care of the elderly in particular have risen as fast as or faster than Social Security expenditures. At current rates of spending, the Medicare program that pays hospital bills will run out of funds in the near future. Some critics of public health care for the elderly suggest the need to ration health care in old age (Callahan 1987). This would mean avoiding expensive treatment of very old people with a short life expectancy and devoting health care resources to younger people with the most productive years ahead of them. Despite the value to society of health care for the young, only the elderly population receives universal health care coverage.

To make these policy changes, advocates of generational inequity emphasize the need for political organizations to counter the influence of advocacy groups for the elderly. In recent decades, the power of old-age interest groups appears to have grown. With skilled leadership and middle-class members, organizations such as the American Association of Retired People (AARP) wield considerable political power. Young families and children have few such powerful organizations representing them in Washington, D.C. Moreover, voting rates of the elderly exceed those of the young. In 1988, for example, 69 percent of people over age 64 voted, whereas 54 percent of people 25 to 44 and 36 percent of people 18 to 24 voted (Torres-Gil 1993).

During the 1980s, one group of politicians and citizens concerned about deficit spending formed an organization called Americans for Generational Equity (AGE) to advocate changing the spending levels of age-based programs. Founded by a Republican senator from Minnesota, AGE questioned the fairness of the treatment of children and the elderly in the

FIGURE 6.2

Returns to Pension Contributions

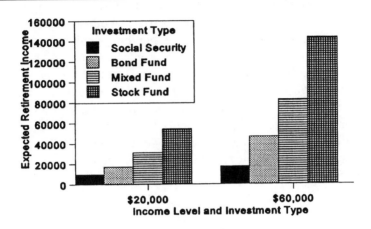

federal budget. The organization attracted members with diverse political beliefs, sponsored conferences and publications, and lobbied legislatures to help define the terms of the debate over public spending (Marshall, Cook, and Marshall 1993; Quadagno 1989).

More recent groups, such as the currently active Concord Coalition and Ross Perot's United We Stand, emphasize the need for deficit reduction, even if it involves lower benefits for older people. Similarly, political advocacy groups comprised of young people, such as Lead or Leave, also concentrate on deficit reduction as a means to reduce future taxes on young generations. Without a major tax increase, the recommendations to reduce the deficit advocated by these groups will likely involve cuts in spending in programs for the elderly.

Opposition to Claims of Generational Inequity

Many view the issue of generational inequity as a threat to the legitimacy of programs for the elderly at a time when both age groups—young and old—need more protection. Opponents of the claims of generational inequity view the elderly and children as equally vulnerable to loss of public support and ultimately as allies rather than competitors in the political process (Kingson, Hirshorn, and Cornman 1986). They note that children and the elderly no more compete with each other for the same government funds than they compete with innumerable other interest groups. Spending for one age group does not reduce spending for other age groups any more than it does for a variety of other programs.

To the contrary, interdependence rather than conflict characterizes generations. Unlike race or gender, a person's age changes. Adults can support the elderly knowing they will receive similar benefits when they become old. Viewed over a whole lifetime rather than in the short term, Social Security spending makes economic sense. Viewed from the long-range perspective of current age as a brief point in the life course, favoring one's own age group at the expense of others makes little sense; each age group has a stake in the well-being of other age groups and the well-being of all members of society (Kingson et al. 1986).

Exaggerations of Generational Inequity

Critics dispute the arguments that on the surface might seem to suggest problems of generational fairness. First, in the area of demography, critics suggest that worries about the growth of the aged population are vastly exaggerated. For example, several European nations, despite having already reached levels of old-age dependency that the United States will not reach for several decades, have not experienced disastrous problems (Myles 1984). Although the size of the aged population has grown in recent decades, leaving more retirees to support, the size of the child population, also in need of support, has declined. The total dependency ratio—the young and old combined relative to the working-age population—peaked in 1964 and has since fallen (Kingson et al. 1986).

Even if demographic trends produce an older population, they do not automatically create greater dependency (Binstock 1994). Improvements in health make it possible for older people to remain productive into later ages than in the past and to continue working beyond the normal retirement age of 65. If the size of the working-age population shrinks relative to the size of the aged population, it would increase employment opportunities for the elderly and partially counter problems of old-age dependency (Uhlenberg 1992). Thus, the number of older people remains less important than the contribution they make to the economy and their needs for public support.

Second, the predictions of looming economic disaster because of deficit spending and rising Social Security and Medicare costs are also exaggerated (Quadagno 1996). Current and future economic investment in the economy and increased rates of savings can generate faster economic growth and higher productivity in the future. The resulting growth in wages can make it easier for workers to support a large elderly population and to reduce the government debt. As Aaron, Bosworth, and Burtless (1989) argue, supporting a large elderly population in the future will produce burdensome problems only if policymakers do nothing now to anticipate the problems. Economic growth and productivity remain more important for the future financial well-being of the country than does the money spent for old-age support.

Third, descriptions of the elderly have exaggerated their political power. Old-age interest groups have little political power compared to interest groups representing business or labor (Wallace et al. 1988). The highly publicized political victories for old-age interest groups have occurred in coalitions with these other interest groups (Williamson, Evans, and Powell 1982). In the future, however, conflict within old-age interest groups may become more important than their united influence; race, ethnicity, class, and gender have the potential to divide the elderly (Torres-Gil 1993).

Even if the elderly do have the political power that many claim, the evidence suggests that they do not use the power to reduce support for children. South (1991) finds only limited support for the claim that states with a large aged population spend less for children. Button and Rosenbaum (1990) find that a large aged population reduces educational spending across counties in Florida from 1973 to 1986. However, this influence has diminished over time, and other factors besides age prove more important as determinants of government spending. If population aging in states and communities does not result in generational conflict and favorable treatment of the elderly relative to children, we should not expect anything different to occur at the national level.

Fourth, data on attitudes fail to affirm claims of political tension or conflict between age groups. Surveys generally reveal that the elderly support spending programs for children (Ponza et al. 1988), and young adults support spending for the elderly (Marshall et al. 1993). Age in general has only a weak relationship with support for public school funding (Vinovskis 1993). Instead, people of the same age have less in common than do people with similar income levels. Because attitudes vary more within age groups than across age groups, it suggests little potential for the emergence of an important age-based political movement now or in the future (Day 1990; Heclo 1988).

One can see the age differences in support for public spending using figures from Vinovskis (1993:56). Figure 6.3 indicates that a majority of

FIGURE 6.3

Public Support for Government Programs

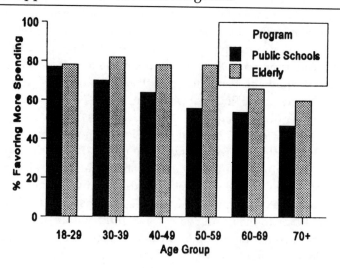

all age groups favor more public spending for both public schools and the elderly. The figure also indicates that all age groups but one (those 18 to 29) favor spending on the elderly more than spending on public schools. Most important, the gap in support for spending on the elderly and public schools appears no larger among people ages 60 and over than it does among people ages 30 to 60. Although older groups less strongly support spending on either program, they do not appear biased in favor of the programs from which they benefit.

Fifth, stereotypes exaggerate the financial well-being of the elderly. Despite high income among a minority of retirees, a substantial percentage of the aged population still has income below the poverty level, and an even larger percentage has income just above the poverty level (Smeeding 1990). Both of these groups remain vulnerable to destitution. Although the elderly on average may be as well off or better off than the nonelderly, the elderly show a larger gap between the poorest and richest than do the nonelderly (Holtz-Eakin and Smeeding 1994). Instead of making crude comparisons across age groups, policymakers should focus on more important differences in economic need based on race, family, class, and labor force status.

Finally, the attention to generational inequity in public spending for children and the elderly ignores the sharing of private resources across generations. Public benefits may favor support of the elderly more than children, but adult children and grandchildren typically receive more private economic support through gifts of time and money from their older parents and grandparents (Kingson et al. 1986). Going beyond finances suggests another form of generational support: Families provide love and companionship that strengthen the bonds between those of different ages. Viewing generational sharing more broadly to include private economic and personal resources moderates the importance of age inequality in government spending.

Generations share common interests in other ways. Although Social Security benefits go primarily to the elderly, they help other generations by reducing the cost and stress of caring for older family members (Minkler 1991). If not supported by the government, older people with inadequate financial resources or poor health would have to depend on family members. Without government support, the costs of private family support—currently, 20 percent of the elderly receive some sort of financial help from adult children (Holtz-Eakin and Smeeding 1994)—would become overwhelming. Moreover, Social Security maintains the independence of older people who would otherwise have to continually ask for help from family members (Kingson et al. 1986). Rather than creating conflict, such public risk protection stabilizes and soothes generational relations.

In summary, supporters of Social Security say critics do not understand the benefits of the system. They note that younger generations have not seen the problems old age presented before the passage of Social Security. If they had, they might have more positive feelings about the program, much like the people described below.

"AT 101, HARVEY MERRILL, a retired Philadelphia stockbroker, is one of the country's oldest Social Security recipients. He firmly believes that people who haven't lived through the economic devastation of a depression cannot truly understand the peace of mind that Social Security brings to the elderly." Although a successful salesman and stockbroker in the 1920s, he suffered during the Depression. With a wife and two young children, Merrill lost his house and savings, and saw a person kill himself in front of his office because of the falling stock market. From his perspective, Social Security was "the most wonderful thing President Roosevelt ever did." Unlike older people 50 years ago, he can relax and enjoy his last years without worrying about where his next check will come from (Lanier 1985:42).

CLAUDE PEPPER, who came to Washington, D.C., as a young senator from Florida in 1936, during the middle of the Great Depression, felt the same way. An enthusiastic supporter of public programs to help those in need, he looked to President Roosevelt and the newly passed Social Security Act as models of good government. After losing in the election of 1950, he practiced law for a decade before running and winning an election for the House of Representatives in 1962 at the age of 61. Until his death in 1989, he used his power in Congress to defend Social Security and the needs of the elderly. Becoming the chairman of the Select Committee on Aging in 1976, "he led successful fights to eliminate the mandatory retirement age of 65, to cut Amtrak fares for senior citizens, and to do away with Social Security penalties for widowed oldsters who chose remarriage rather than living together." During the 1980s, he would receive "up to 200 calls and 400 letters a day—not just from the nation's elderly, but from widows, orphans and the disabled who depend on Social Security benefits." He has consistently and vigorously fought proposals to cut Social Security benefits. At a time when criticisms of Social Security began to grow, he said, "I refuse to believe that a country as rich and powerful as ours cannot guarantee the basic comfort of its older citizens. . . . We ought to leave Social Security just as it is" (Langdon 1982:38).

Real Sources of Concern

The evidence of exaggerated claims of generational inequity raises an important question: Why have the public concerns about fairness in the treatment of children and the elderly come to dominate public policy debates despite the arguments against them? Some critics view claims of generational inequity as examples of ageism. The elderly have simply become a convenient scapegoat for broader social and economic problems (Binstock 1983). Ageist attitudes show in stereotypes of selfish and affluent older people who unfairly gain from public spending. Such hostility and blame correspond to racism in the treatment of other minority groups. Both ageism and racism involve forms of blaming the victim (Minkler 1991).

Other critics view arguments for generational inequity as efforts of business groups to limit government spending. Rather than a conflict between young and old, the debate involves conflict between social classes (Quadagno 1989). The expansion of public support for the elderly and other groups combined with higher taxes to fund the programs reflect a loss of political power and reduced potential for profits among corporate owners and leaders (Walker 1993). Yet framing the issue in terms of support for children relative to the elderly sounds better than framing the issue in terms of the economic needs of business. In reality, the debate remains essentially an aspect of class conflict according to supporters of old-age programs.

The publicity campaigns of a few small but influential and conservative interest groups contributed to the exaggerated concerns about generational inequity. In response to expansion of the welfare state in the 1970s, conservative intellectuals funded by business groups launched an attack on welfare programs (Edsall 1984), in part by highlighting the issue of generational inequity. Quadagno (1989) claims that Americans for Generational Equity, a major force behind the publicity campaign, "created the notion that the problem of inadequate social resources for children was a product of excessive benefits for the aged" (p. 354).

Such efforts to produce a political split between interests representing children and the elderly generally failed to reach their goal. Ties across generations remain strong, and support for Social Security continues among all age groups. Still, debates about generational inequity have had some influence on policy. For example, the concern of policymakers with generational inequity affected legislation for the coverage of catastrophic health care costs among the elderly in the late 1980s. Medicare provisions for the elderly do not cover prolonged health problems or short-term, but hugely expensive, health costs. A proposed expansion of Medicare would have covered hospital and medical costs for catastrophic illnesses, expanded payments for long-term nursing home care, and provided new benefits for prescription drugs (Wallace et al. 1988). The changes would help prevent serious illness from impoverishing elderly people.

However, opposition to raising taxes on young families to support such a program led legislators to develop a new funding strategy. Rather than having workers contribute to supporting the elderly now in return for support when they became old, the legislation taxed high-income elderly and required higher Medicare payments from the elderly. Opposition to a system that made transfers across classes in old age instead of across ages led to the repeal of the legislation (Holstein and Minkler 1991). Affluent elderly who had little need for the public benefits resisted paying for others, thus dividing older people across class lines (Pierson and Smith 1994). Because class redistribution generally gains less popular support than generational redistribution, the program had little chance for success.

To avoid these kinds of problems, and to limit the concerns about fair treatment of children and the elderly, new programs will need to help people of all ages. Advocates of older people should likewise broaden their agenda to support programs that link family members of all generations (Kingson 1988). For example, efforts to provide support for catastrophic health expenses among the elderly might include provisions for medical leave for workers to care at home for both children and elderly family members (Wisensale 1988). The more policies can highlight ties across generations, the wider the support they will gain.

The Historical Context of Debates over Generational Inequity

Whatever the arguments favoring and opposing generational inequity, the fact that the debate exists indicates changes in relationships across generations. Although tensions between the young and old have always existed, generational relationships change with social and historical conditions (Achenbaum 1993). Older generations desire to keep what they have known in the past, whereas younger generations desire to change existing institutions. Balancing stability and change, both necessary to the survival of society, creates problems of generational conflict (Bengtson and Murray 1993). Yet only recently has such conflict emerged as an important political problem.

As mentioned earlier, generational conflict in colonial America often involved resentment of the young over the power and wealth of older generations (Fischer 1978). As the owners of a community's most important economic resource—land—older people had power and respect unavailable to younger people. Young adults had to wait for their parents to die before obtaining their own property. The industrial revolution, however, reduced the importance of land as a source of wealth and gave advantages to younger innovators in the industrial economy. During the 1800s, power and prestige of the elderly eroded, whereas work opportunities and income of younger age groups expanded.

Over the past century, a system of support emerged to care for the elderly in industrial societies. The system created obligations for an adult generation to raise a younger generation in exchange for public and private support decades later when the older generation reached retirement age and the younger generation reached working age (Bengtson and Murray 1993). Such ties across generations created solidarity within families and moderated the potential for conflict across age groups. If supporting the elderly imposed costs on adults during their working lives, it also promised some benefits when they reached old age. From this perspective, Social Security merely involved formalizing family sharing: The government would collect taxes now from workers to pay current retirees, and collect taxes from future workers to pay future retirees.

Only recently have social and demographic changes threatened the logic of the generational contract and sharpened the potential for conflict across generations (Bengtson and Murray 1993). Smaller families, rising divorce rates, and increased dependence of individuals and families on government programs rather than on other family members raised the costs of the contract to new and smaller generations. Where young generations at one time could expect to support their older parents, they now can expect to also support older grandparents and great-grandparents. The longer length of life not only increases the costs but limits the personal contact between younger generations and the older generations they have to support.

Consider some examples that suggest how emerging family structures can change the nature of the relationship across generations.

MARY WAS THE PRODUCT of a decision of her parents late in life to have another child. Her father, age 50 when she was born, died before she finished college. Her mother, age 40 at Mary's birth, was separated by four decades from her youngest child. Now that Mary has reached 40 herself, she faces a problem. At the same time her children need time and money, her 80-year-old mother needs the same. The mothers of Mary's friends are still relatively young, around 65 and 70, and are able to care for themselves. Because her mother, like many other women these days, postponed childbearing to a late age, Mary has to simultaneously juggle care for older and younger generations that both need her attention and time.

BECAUSE HIS MOTHER IS 25 YEARS OLDER than he is, Bill faces a different problem. He has just reached age 65 and looks forward to leisure after a lifetime of working and caring for children. However, his mother has now reached 90 years of age and also needs help. Unlike Mary, Bill could finish raising his children before having to worry about caring for his mother. Still, because his mother lived to such an old age, Bill has new family responsibilities. Although he would like to travel and perhaps spend the winter in Arizona, the need to stay close to his mother prevents him from doing so. Furthermore, at a time when he has to make do with modest retirement income, Bill must contribute financially to his mother.

With changing levels of fertility and mortality, such patterns of care for older parents have become increasingly common and have changed the nature of generational relations in recent decades.

The National Context of Debates over Generational Inequity

Along with historical context, national context affects the emergence of issues of generational fairness. Despite experiencing similar population changes, other high-income nations have not experienced the same generational tensions as the United States. Indeed, no other nation besides the United States so clearly frames spending issues in terms of funding for the elderly relative to funding for children (Myles and Quadagno 1991). Even in Canada, our closest neighbor, debates over generational inequity did not occur. A search of computer databases for references to generational inequity in scholarly and popular publications in both Canada and the United States found many in the American literature but few in the Canadian literature (Marshall et al. 1993) .

Why the differences in policy debates between two otherwise demographically and economically similar nations? Likely of prime importance is the structure of the welfare programs in the two nations. Compared to the United States, Canada offers somewhat less generous, but more universal, public pension benefits. Unlike the United States, Canada also offers modest, but again universal, family allowance benefits to families with children. As discussed earlier, universal programs tend to create solidarity among recipients, and universal programs common to both the elderly and children tend to create solidarity across generations (Myles and Quadagno 1994; Marshall et al. 1993). In the United States, the existence of social insurance programs for the elderly contrasts with the less popular and successful social assistance programs for children.

Spending for Children and the Elderly

To understand national sources of generational inequity, we need to compare public spending on the elderly to public spending on children. Some nations may spend little on pensions but may also spend little on children. Other nations may spend generously on both groups, and still other nations may spend relatively more on one group than the other. We need some type of measure of national standing that contrasts public spending for the two age groups (O'Higgins 1988).

More specifically, a measure of age differences in public spending might compare public pensions and family allowances. Pension expenditures represent the major source of public support for the elderly. Family allowance expenditures represent an analogous program for children.

Both pensions and family allowances define eligibility primarily on the basis of age rather than need: Families with children under approximately age 18 receive family allowances, and people over approximately age 65 receive pensions. Both pensions and family allowances provide regular cash benefits to individuals or families and present comparable, easily understandable figures for the high-income nations.

Averaged across all nations, spending on family allowances slightly exceeds 1 percent of gross domestic product (GDP). In contrast, spending on pensions reaches nearly 8 percent of GDP. Moreover, in no nation does family allowance spending exceed pension spending (International Labour Organization 1989). Because the elderly depend heavily on public support through pensions, whereas children depend on family allowances only as a supplement to private family income, we cannot expect equality between the two programs. Yet the degree of the gap in spending for the two programs can vary across nations.

To compare national differences more precisely, Table 6.1 takes family allowance spending as a percentage of both family allowance and pension spending. The mean equals 11.8—just over one-tenth goes to family allowances and the other nine-tenths to pensions. In comparison to other high-income nations, nations with percentage spending on family allowances well above this average would appear to favor children in their public programs, and nations with percentage spending on family allowances well below this average would appear to favor older people.

Because the United States lacks a family allowance program and depends completely on private support, educational expenditures, tax benefits, and need-based assistance for support of children, it has the lowest possible value of zero on the measure of relative spending. Even with the other programs added in, the United States still ranks low in public spending on children relative to the elderly (Pampel 1994). Although Japan and Switzerland have family allowance programs, their spending levels barely exceed those of the United States. At the other extreme, Belgium and France devote nearly one-fourth of total family allowance and pension spending to family allowances. Other Catholic nations, such as Austria and Ireland, also devote relatively more to children than to the elderly. Pro-child traditions in most Catholic nations seem to produce generous support for families with children.

The high spending on children in France, for example, shows in the following example:

MARRIED BEFORE FINISHING their advanced degrees, Cecile and Francois now work for the French government and live in a town of nearly

TABLE 6.1

National Differences in Spending
for Children and the Elderly: 1986

Nation	Family Allowances	Public Pension	% Family Allowances
Belgium	2.42	6.75	26.4
France	3.09	9.22	25.1
United Kingdom	1.27	5.77	18.0
Canada	0.83	3.83	17.8
Austria	2.30	10.80	17.6
Ireland	1.11	5.61	16.5
Netherlands	1.88	11.30	14.3
Australia	0.65	3.97	14.1
Norway	1.07	8.14	11.6
Sweden	1.38	12.40	10.0
West Germany	0.71	9.25	7.1
Finland	0.72	10.30	6.5
New Zealand	0.54	9.44	5.4
Denmark	0.40	7.66	5.0
Italy	0.61	12.30	4.7
Japan	0.05	3.78	1.3
Switzerland	0.04	7.61	0.5
United States	0.00	4.30	0.0
Mean	1.06	7.91	11.8

400,000 people about 100 miles from Paris. As the parents of two children, they receive $70 a month in family allowance benefits. Also, because they both work for the government, they get a supplemental benefit of $100 a month to help raise children. Because the youngest child is under 3 years old and Cecile works part-time, they get another $300 a month for child care; the French government provides this benefit in the hope that supporting part-time work creates more job opportunities and lowers unemployment. The older child, age 5, goes to a free preschool before he enters public school next year. Finally, and also as a means to help reduce unemployment, the French government gives them $120 a month and some tax deductions for hiring an in-home baby-sitter. The expenses of raising children add up quickly, but the *variety of support that Cecile and Francois receive from the government reduces the costs substantially. If they decide to have another child, the national social security system will cover the bulk of prenatal, delivery, and postpartum expenses. For a third child, mothers are guaranteed a six-month paid maternity leave, two months longer than for prior pregnancies, to cover the added responsibility of an expanding family (Smolowe, 1992). Furthermore, their family allowance benefit will increase from $70 to somewhere around $250 a month. Although unheard of in the United States, French parents take these benefits for granted, much the way older people take public pensions for granted.*

Comparing family allowance and pension spending reveals another interesting result. In general, nations that spend highly on pensions also spend relatively highly on family allowances, and vice versa. Thus, high-spending nations, such as Sweden, tend to support both children and the elderly more than do low-spending nations, such as the United States. Rather than competition, where high spending for one program means low spending for the other, the figures tend to show similarities across countries. Such results contradict the claims of generational inequity that public support for older people lowers support for children.

Comparing trends over time in spending for the two programs for these nations also contradicts claims of generational inequity. All of the high-income nations have experienced an increase in the percentage of the population age 65 and over and a decline in the percentage of the population under age 15 (Pampel 1994). Despite the population trends, family allowance benefits have increased in most nations, again indicating that population aging does not automatically mean reduced spending for children. For example, France intentionally increased family allowance benefits as a means to encourage childbearing and larger families. Sweden also increased family allowance spending in response to population aging as a means to equalize the relative economic standing of the two groups. In both cases, population aging indirectly produced more spending on children rather than less.

Sources of Relative Spending on Children and the Elderly

Although generally inconsistent with claims of generational inequity, the figures demonstrate that some nations spend relatively more on older people than on children. In the United States in particular, these spending differences have produced tensions over generational fairness. What characteristics might explain national differences in age-based spending and in generational tensions?

Political factors likely play an important role. Some nations have a political environment in which competition exists among a large number of diverse and specialized interest groups. Groups defined by age as well as region, class, industry, gender, and other characteristics compete for political power and beneficial policies. Given their specialized interests, these groups attempt to influence policy relevant to narrowly defined goals and specific programs. In such an environment, the elderly and children may develop distinct and perhaps even competing interests. Furthermore, as the populations age in these nations, group size as a political asset comes to favor the elderly and to disadvantage children and families.

In other nations, the political environment shows more conflict between social classes. As discussed in the previous chapter, even spending for age-based programs like pensions results from the distribution of power among social classes. The importance of class-based power in some nations tends to restrain the importance of age groups. If class membership represents the dominant social, economic, and political division, then conflict based on age would remain relatively insignificant. In fact, a welfare state based on bargaining among social classes would favor redistribution to both young and old within classes and thereby minimizes age competition.

These political environments correspond roughly to the types of pension regimes discussed in the previous chapter. Competition among diverse interest groups, sometimes including the elderly, most likely emerges in liberal regimes like the United States. In these nations, where program benefits closely match contributions, groups tend to try to expand or preserve their own particular benefits. Compared to other liberal nations, however, the system of checks and balances in the United States encourages even more strongly the formation and activity of special interest groups. Competition between age groups is least likely to emerge in social democratic nations such as Sweden. Here, universal programs provide for both children and the elderly, and class unity overshadows age differences.

Conclusion

Despite the presence of conflict between generations throughout history, debates of fairness between the young and old have taken a new turn in recent decades with the unprecedented growth of the aged population. Those concerned with generational inequity believe that population aging has increased the political influence, public pension benefits, and economic affluence of the elderly. The same demographic trends have reduced the political influence, public welfare benefits, and economic well-being of children. In terms of policy, legislators should therefore limit spending growth in Social Security and Medicare programs for the elderly and redirect some of the funds to programs for children. Perhaps most important, legislators should reduce deficit spending and the debt that future generations of young people and workers will have to repay.

Few disagree with the direction of the trends, but many debate the causes and implications of the trends. Critics claim that political ideology underlies the generational inequity thesis. Conservatives and business interests opposed to current levels of taxes and welfare spending have used worries about population aging to hide the common interests of children and the elderly in public support. Critics support expanded spending for children along with continued support for the elderly. Although such support requires higher taxes, the benefits will far outweigh the harm. Having proven themselves as highly successful and popular programs, Social Security and Medicare deserve protection rather than dismantlement.

Critics also point to the organization of programs for the elderly as a source of generational inequity. Universal and social insurance programs gain widespread support, but social assistance or need-based programs do not. In nations with universal programs, public support for both children and the elderly remain popular despite growth of the aged population. In nations like the United States, where children depend on social assistance programs, support for more popular pension programs rises and support for children's programs falls.

If nothing else, the debates over generational inequity highlight the importance of generational membership for experiences in old age. Those entering old age in recent decades have enjoyed benefits that improved substantially over the benefits received by earlier generations reaching old age. Yet the generations reaching old age in the next century will confront strong pressures to cut benefits. The financial well-being of the elderly in decades to come will depend on policy changes made in the next several years. Whatever the outcome, the changes illustrate how generational membership contributes to the experiences people have in old age.

Epilogue

The sociology of aging or the field of gerontology covers numerous topics, including microlevel issues involving individual well-being, social support, retirement satisfaction, religious beliefs, personal adjustment, interpersonal relations, and nursing home care. This text has focused instead on macrolevel issues of group differences, national policies, and social changes. It argues that larger forces related to the degree of inequality, the structure of populations, and the nature of political values shape individual experiences of growing old in important ways. A subject as broad as aging can benefit from multiple perspectives, and the one presented here should complement others.

The macrolevel perspective relates closely to larger trends in theory and research in the field of sociology. Sociology in recent decades has attended more to the diversity of social positions and experiences across class, race, ethnic, and gender groups; to the political bases of social inequality; and to the differences across nations and societies. Applied to aging, a sociological perspective directs attention to the same sort of issues. This text has (a) identified inequality in old age across class, race, ethnic, and gender groups; (b) related that inequality to social policy in the United States; and (c) compared inequality among the aged population across high-income nations with different political institutions and public policies.

A key theme to emerge from the previous chapters is that inequality exists not only between the young, middle-aged, and old, but it also exists within these age groups. This theme implies varied experiences across groups of elderly people in different positions in the stratification system, and it warns against crude generalizations about the elderly. Such generalizations have some uses. In simple terms, they can emphasize that all old people share certain characteristics, experiences, and roles by virtue of the social images and stereotypes people have about the elderly. Yet used carelessly, such generalizations can mask variation within age groups. Previous chapters have shown how aging can vary by social class and by ascriptive statuses, such as race, ethnicity, gender, national citizenship, and generational membership. These variations in aging emphasize the importance of diversity and inequality among the elderly.

Diversity and inequality in old age become particularly clear when viewed from a life course perspective. Because they exist before old age, diversity and inequality can be studied by comparing changes over the life course from middle age to old age. Some perspectives suggest that old age reduces the inequality that exists at earlier ages, whereas other perspectives suggest that old age maintains or increases that inequality. Such claims need testing with longitudinal data that follow individuals and cohorts over time into old age rather than with cross-sectional data that compare different age groups at one time point. My review of the longitudinal data reveals considerable complexity, but with more support for status maintenance and diversity than for status equalization or leveling. Regardless of the results, however, the use of a life course perspective that views old age as in part a continuation of earlier life experiences adds much to our understanding.

The comparison of the status of the elderly with the status of children can likewise benefit from a perspective on aging and the life course. Discussion of generational inequity typically focuses on the improved status of current older people relative to current youth. Critics of the thesis, however, suggest that such claims of age group competition miss the life course links between these age groups: Younger generations have a stake in supporting the elderly because they will grow old and will need pension support later. To the extent that current debates about the well-being of children and the elderly ignore these types of life course connections, they fail to understand the social nature of aging.

The potential for different experiences during the transition from middle age to old age and for different relationships across generations also shows in comparative evidence. The nature and degree of diversity and inequality in old age differ crucially across nations with different political institutions and public pension systems. The level and interpretation of inequality between the young and old likewise differ crucially across nations with different political institutions and social welfare programs. This national diversity indicates that the characteristics within and between age groups result from conscious public policy choices. Cross-national comparisons, like comparisons across the life course, thus offer a useful perspective on the particular experiences in the United States that we tend to take for granted.

Together, variation in aging across classes, race, ethnic and gender groups, nations, and generations highlights the contingent social nature of old age rather than physical or biological characteristics of old age. If many of the experiences of old age result from socially created images, structures of inequality, and institutions of public support, then the problems we treat as the inevitable result of growing old are actually amenable to change. Although such change may prove difficult in practice, the sociological perspective on aging emphasizes the possibility of making improvements.

References

Aaron, Henry J., Barry P. Bosworth, and Gary Burtless. 1989. *Can America Afford to Grow Old? Paying for Social Security*. Washington, DC: The Brookings Institution.

Achenbaum, W. A. 1993. "Generational Relations in Historical Context." Pp. 25-42 in *The Changing Contract across Generations*, edited by Vern L. Bengtson and W. Andrew Achenbaum. New York: Aldine de Gruyter.

Angel, J. L., R. J. Angel, J. L. McClelland, and K. S. Markides. 1996. "Nativity, Declining Health, and Preferences in Living Arrangements among Elderly Mexican-Americans: Implications for Long-Term Care." *The Gerontologist* 36:464-73.

Angel, R. J. and M. Tienda. 1982. "Determinants of Extended Household Structure: Cultural Pattern or Economic Need?" *American Journal of Sociology* 87:1360-83.

Baldwin, Peter. 1990. *The Politics of Social Solidarity: Class Bases of the European Welfare State 1875-1975*. Cambridge, UK: Cambridge University Press.

Belgrave, L. L., M. L. Wykle, and J. M. Choi. 1993. "Health, Double Jeopardy, and Culture: The Use of Institutionalization by African-Americans." *The Gerontologist* 33:379-85.

Bengtson, V. L. and T. M. Murray. 1993. "Justice across Generations (and Cohorts): Sociological Perspectives on the Life Course and Reciprocities over Time." Pp. 111-38 in *Justice across Generations: What Does It Mean?* edited by Lee M. Cohen. Washington, DC: Public Policy Institute, American Association of Retired Persons.

Berkman, L., B. Singer, and K. Manton. 1989. "Black/White Differences in Health Status and Mortality among the Elderly." *Demography* 26:661-78.

Berkowitz, Edward D. and Kim McQuaid. 1992. *Creating the Welfare State: The Political Economy of Twentieth Century Reform*. Lawrence: University of Kansas Press.

Bernstein, Merton C. and Joan Brodshaug Bernstein. 1988. *Social Security: The System That Works*. New York: Basic Books.

Binstock, Robert H. 1983. "The Aged as Scapegoat." *The Gerontologist* 12:265-80.

———. 1994. "Transcending Intergenerational Equity." Pp. 155-87 in *Economic Security and Intergenerational Justice: A Look at North America*, edited by Theodore R. Marmor, Timothy M. Smeeding, and Vernon L. Greene. Washington, DC: Urban Institute.

Blakemore, Ken and Margaret Boneham. 1994. *Age, Race, and Ethnicity: A Comparative Approach*. Philadelphia: Open University Press.

Bradshaw, York W. and Michael Wallace. 1996. *Global Inequalities*. Thousand Oaks, CA: Pine Forge Press.

Burgess, Ernest W. and Harvey J. Locke. 1945. *The Family: From Institution to Companionship*. New York: American Press.

Burkhauser, R. V. and G. J. Duncan. 1988. "Life Events, Public Policy, and the Economic Vulnerability of Children and the Elderly." Pp. 29-54 in *The Vulnerable*, edited by John L. Palmer, Timothy Smeeding, and Barbara Boyle Torrey. Washington, DC: Urban Institute.

Burkhauser, R. V., G. J. Duncan, and R. Hauser. 1994. "Sharing Prosperity across the Age Distribution: A Comparison of the United States and Germany in the 1980s." *The Gerontologist* 34:150-60.

Burr, J. A., M. M. Massagli, J. E. Mutchler, and A. M. Pienta. 1996. "Labor Force Transitions among Older African American and White Men." *Social Forces* 74:963-82.

Burr, J. A. and J. E. Mutchler. 1993. "Nativity, Acculturation, and Economic Status: Explanations of Asian American Living Arrangements in Later Life." *Journal of Gerontology* 48:S55-63.

———. 1994. "Ethnic Living Arrangements: Cultural Convergence or Cultural Manifestation?" *Social Forces* 72:169-79.

Burton, L. M., P. Dilworth-Anderson, and V. L. Bengtson. 1992. "Creating Culturally Relevant Ways of Thinking about Diversity and Aging: Theoretical Challenges for the Twenty-First Century." Pp. 129-40 in *Diversity: New Approaches to Ethnic Minority Aging*, edited by E. Percil Stanford and Fernando M. Torres-Gil. Amityville, NY: Baywood.

Butler, Robert. 1975. *Why Survive? Being Old in America*. New York: Harper & Row.

Button, J. and W. Rosenbaum. 1990. "Gray Power, Gray Peril, or Gray Myth? The Political Impact of the Aging in Local Sunbelt Politics." *Social Science Quarterly* 71:25-38.

Calasanti, T. M. 1993. "Bringing Diversity: Toward an Inclusive Theory of Retirement." *Journal of Aging Studies* 7:133-50.

———. 1996. "Incorporating Diversity: Meaning, Levels of Research, and Implications for Theory." *The Gerontologist* 36:147-56.

Calasanti, T. M. and A. Bonanno. 1992. "Working 'Over-Time': Economic Restructuring and Retirement of a Class." *Sociological Quarterly* 33:135-52.

Callahan, Daniel. 1987. *Setting Limits: Medical Goals in an Aging Society*. New York: Simon and Schuster.

Cates, Jerry R. 1983. *Insuring Inequality: Administrative Leadership in Social Security, 1935-1954*. Ann Arbor: University of Michigan Press.

Christensen, K. 1990. "Bridges over Troubled Water: How Older Workers View the Labor Market." Pp. 175-208 in *Bridges to Retirement: Older Workers in a Changing Labor Market,* edited by Peter B. Doeringer. Ithaca, NY: ILR Press.

Clark, D. and G. Maddox. 1993. "Race, Aging, and Functional Health: Evidence of Selective Survival?" *Journal of Aging and Health* 54:536-57.

Clark, R. L., L. S. Ghent, and A. E. Headen. 1994. "Retiree Health Insurance and Pension Coverage: Variation by Firm Characteristics." *Journal of Gerontology: Social Sciences* 49:S53-61.

Clark, William F., Anabel O. Pelham, and Marleen L. Clark. 1988. *Old and Poor: A Critical Assessment of the Low-Income Elderly.* Lexington, MA: Lexington Books.

Clarke, C. J. and L. J. Neidert. 1992. "Living Arrangements of the Elderly: An Examination of Differences According to Ancestry and Generation." *The Gerontologist* 32:796-804.

Cohen, Wilbur and Milton Friedman. 1972. *Social Security: Universal or Selective?* Washington, DC: American Enterprise Institute.

Coupland, Douglas. 1991. *Generation X: Tales for an Accelerated Culture.* New York: St. Martin's.

Cowgill, Donald O. 1986. *Aging around the World.* Belmont, CA: Wadsworth.

Cowgill, Donald O. and Lowell D. Holmes. 1972. *Aging and Modernization.* New York: Appleton-Century-Crofts.

Crimmins, E. M., M. D. Hayward, and Y. Saito. 1994. "Changing Mortality and Morbidity Rates and the Health Status and Life Expectancy of the Older Population." *Demography* 31:159-75.

Crimmins, E. M., Y. Saito, and S. L. Reynolds. 1997. "Further Evidence on Recent Trends in the Prevalence and Incidence of Disability among Older Americans from Two Sources: The LSOA and the NHIS." *Journal of Gerontology: Social Sciences* 52B:S59-71.

Crowley, J. E. 1985. "Longitudinal Effects of Retirement on Men's Psychological and Physical Well-Being." Pp. 147-74 in *Retirement among American Men,* edited by Herbert S. Parnes, Joan E. Crowley, R. Jean Haurin, William R. Morgan, Frank L. Mott, and Gilbert Nestel. Lexington, MA: Lexington Books.

Crystal, S. 1982. *America's Old Age Crisis: Public Policy and the Two Worlds of Aging.* New York: Basic Books.

Crystal, S. and D. Shea. 1990a. "The Economic Well-Being of the Elderly." *Review of Income and Wealth* 36:227-47.

———. 1990b. "Cumulative Advantage, Cumulative Disadvantage, and Inequality among Elderly People." *The Gerontologist* 30:437-43.

Crystal, S., D. Shea, and S. Krishnaswami. 1992. "Educational Attainment, Occupational History, and Stratification: Determinants of Later-Life Economic Outcomes." *Journal of Gerontology: Social Sciences* 47:S213-21.

Crystal, S. and K. Waehrer. 1996. "Later-Life Economic Inequality in Longitudinal Perspective." *Journal of Gerontology: Social Sciences* 51B:S307-18.

Curtin, Sharon R. 1972. *Nobody Ever Died of Old Age.* Boston: Little, Brown.

Dannefer, D. 1987. "Aging as Intracohort Differentiation: Accentuation, the Matthew Effect, and the Life Course." *Sociological Forum* 2:211-36.

Day, Christine L. 1990. *What Older Americans Think: Interest Groups and Aging Policy.* Princeton, NJ: Princeton University Press.

Delany, Sarah and A. Elizabeth Delany. 1993. *Having Our Say: The Delany Sisters' First 100 Years.* New York: Kodansha International.

Doeringer, Peter B., ed. 1990. *Bridges to Retirement: Older Workers in a Changing Labor Market.* Ithaca, NY: ILR Press.

Dowd, J. J. and V. L. Bengtson. 1978. "Aging in Minority Populations: An Examination of the Double Jeopardy Hypothesis." *Journal of Gerontology* 33:427-36.

Duleep, H. O. 1989. "Measuring Socioeconomic Mortality Differentials over Time." *Demography* 26:345-51.

Duncan, G. J. and K. R. Smith. 1989. "The Rising Affluence of the Elderly: How Far, How Fair, and How Frail?" *Annual Review of Sociology* 15:261-89.

Duneier, Mitchell. 1992. *Slim's Table: Race, Respectability, and Masculinity.* Chicago: University of Chicago Press.

Edsall, Thomas B. 1984. *The New Politics of Inequality.* New York: Norton.

Elder, G. H., Jr. and A. M. O'Rand. 1995. "Adult Lives in a Changing Society." Pp. 452-75 in *Sociological Perspectives on Social Psychology,* edited by Karen S. Cook, Gary Alan Fine, and James S. House. Needham Heights, MA: Allyn and Bacon.

Elder, G. H. and E. K. Pavalko. 1993. "Work Careers in Men's Later Years: Transitions, Trajectories, and Historical Change." *Journal of Gerontology: Social Sciences* 48:S180-91.

Elo, I. T. and S. H. Preston. 1994. "Estimating African-American Mortality from Inaccurate Data." *Demography* 31:427-58.

Esping-Andersen, Gøsta. 1989. "The Three Political Economies of the Welfare State." *Canadian Review of Sociology and Anthropology* 26:10-35.

———. 1990. *The Three Worlds of Welfare Capitalism.* Princeton, NJ: Princeton University Press.

Estes, Carroll L. 1979. *The Aging Enterprise.* San Francisco: Jossey-Bass.

———. 1993. "The Aging Enterprise Revisited." *The Gerontologist* 33:292-98.

Evans, Peter B., Dietrich Reuschemeyer, and Theda Skocpol, eds. 1985. *Bringing the State Back in.* New York: Cambridge University Press.

Ferraro, K. F. and M. A. Farmer. 1996. "Double Jeopardy to Health Hypothesis for African Americans: Analysis and Critique." *Journal of Health and Social Behavior* 37:27-43.

Fischer, David Hackett. 1978. *Growing Old in America.* Oxford, UK: Oxford University Press.

Franklin, Jon. 1986. *Writing for Story.* New York: Atheneum.

Freed, Anne O. 1992. *The Changing Worlds of Older Women in Japan.* Manchester, CT: Knowledge, Ideas & Trends.

Fries, J. 1980. "Aging, Natural Death, and the Compression of Mortality." *New England Journal of Medicine* 303:130-36.

———. 1982. "Compression of Morbidity: Near or Far?" *Milbank Quarterly* 67:208-32.

Gelfand, Donald E. 1994. *Aging and Ethnicity: Knowledge and Services.* New York: Springer.

Gendell, M. and J. S. Siegel. 1996. "Trends in Retirement Age in the United States, 1955-1993, by Sex and Race." *Journal of Gerontology: Social Sciences* 51B:S132-39.

Gibson, R. C. 1987. "Reconceptualizing Retirement for Black Americans." *The Gerontologist* 27:691-98.

———. 1994. "The Age-by-Race Gap in Health and Mortality in the Older Population: A Social Science Research Agenda." *The Gerontologist* 34:454-62.

Giddings, Paula. 1984. *When and Where I Enter: The Impact of Black Women on Race and Sex in America.* New York: Bantam.

Gratton, B. 1987. "Familism among Black and Mexican-American Elderly: Myth or Reality?" *Journal of Aging Studies* 1:19-32.

Grigsby, J. S. 1996. "The Meaning of Heterogeneity: An Introduction." *The Gerontologist* 36:141-44.

Haber, Carole and Brian Gratton. 1994. *Old Age and the Search for Security: An American Social History.* Bloomington: Indiana University Press.

Harpaz, B. J. 1997. "Older Immigrants Frantic about Loss of Benefits." *Boulder Daily Camera*, March 24, p. 6A-1.

Harrington, Michael. 1962. *The Other America.* New York: Macmillan.

———. 1984. *The New American Poverty.* New York: Viking Penguin.

Hayward, M. D., S. Friedman, and H. Chen. 1996. "Race Inequities in Men's Retirement." *Journal of Gerontology: Social Sciences* 51B:S1-10.

Hayward, M. D. and W. R. Grady. 1990. "Work and Retirement among a Cohort of Older Men in the United States, 1966-1983." *Demography* 27:337-56.

Hayward, M. D., W. R. Grady, M. A. Hardy, and D. Somers. 1989. "Occupational Influences on Retirement, Disability, and Death." *Demography* 26:393-409.

Hayward, M. D., M. A. Hardy, and M. Liu. 1994. "Work after Retirement: The Experiences of Older Men in the United States." *Social Science Research* 23:82-107.

Heclo, H. 1988. "Generational Politics." Pp. 381-412 in *The Vulnerable*, edited by John L. Palmer, Timothy Smeeding, and Barbara Boyle Torrey. Washington, DC: Urban Institute.

Hennessy, C. H. and R. John. 1995. "The Interpretation of Burden among Pueblo Indian Caregivers." *Journal of Aging Studies* 9:215-29.

Henretta, J. C. 1992. "Uniformity and Diversity: Life Course Institutionalization and Late-Life Work Exit." *Sociological Quarterly* 33:265-79.

Henretta, J. C. and R. T. Campbell. 1976. "Status Attainment and Status Maintenance: A Study of Stratification in Old Age." *American Sociological Review*
41:981-92.

Himes, C. L., D. P. Hogan, and D. J. Eggebeen. 1996. "Living Arrangements of
Minority Elders." *Journal of Gerontology: Social Sciences* 51B:S542-48.

Himes, C. L., S. H. Preston, and G. A. Condran. 1994. "A Relational Model of
Mortality at Older Ages in Low Mortality Countries." *Population Studies*
48:269-91.

Holden, K. C. and H. D. Kuo. 1996. "Complex Marital Histories and Economic
Well-Being: The Continuing Legacy of Divorce and Widowhood as the HRS
Cohort Approaches Retirement." *The Gerontologist* 36:383-90.

Holden, K. C. and P. J. Smock. 1991. "The Economic Costs of Marital Disrup-
tion: Why Do Women Bear a Disproportionate Cost?" *Annual Review of Sociology* 17:51-78.

Holstein, M. and M. Minkler. 1991. "The Short Life and Painful Death of Medicare Catastrophic Coverage Act." Pp. 189-208 in *Critical Perspectives on Aging: The Political and Moral Economy of Growing Old,* edited by Meredith
Minkler and Carroll L. Estes. Amityville, NY: Baywood.

Holtz-Eakin, D. and T. M. Smeeding. 1994. "Income, Wealth, and Intergenerational Economic Relations of the Aged." Pp. 102-45 in *Demography of Aging,*
edited by Linda G. Martin and Samuel H. Preston. Washington, DC: National Academy Press.

Huber, E., C. Ragin, and J. D. Stephens. 1993. "Social Democracy, Constitutional Structure, and the Welfare State." *American Journal of Sociology* 99:711-49.

Hurd, M. D. 1990. "Research on the Elderly: Economic Status, Retirement, Consumption, and Savings." *Journal of Economic Literature* 28:565-637.

International Labour Office. 1989. *The Cost of Social Security.* Geneva, Switzerland: International Labour Office.

Johnson, Colleen L. and Barbara M. Barer. 1997. *Life beyond 85 Years: The Aura of
Survivorship.* New York: Springer.

Kamerman, Sheila B. and Alfred J. Kahn. 1988. "Social Policy and Children in
the United States and Europe." Pp. 351-80 in *The Vulnerable,* edited by John
L. Palmer, Timothy Smeeding, and Barbara Boyle Torrey. Washington, DC:
Urban Institute.

Kanin, Garson. 1978. *It Takes a Long Time to Become Young.* Garden City, NY:
Doubleday.

Katzenstein, Peter S. 1985. *Small States in World Markets: Industrial Policy in
Europe.* Ithaca, NY: Cornell University Press.

Kerr, Clark. 1983. *The Future of Industrial Societies: Convergence or Continuing Diversity?* Cambridge, MA: Harvard University Press.

Kingson, E. R. 1988. "Generational Equity: An Unexpected Opportunity to
Broaden the Politics of Aging." *The Gerontologist* 28:765-72.

Kingson, Eric R. and Edward D. Berkowitz. 1993. *Social Security and Medicare: A Policy Primer.* Westport, CT: Auburn House.

Kingson, Eric R., Barbara A. Hirshorn, and John M. Cornman. 1986. *Ties That Bind: The Interdependence of Generations.* Washington, DC: Seven Locks Press.

Kinoshita, Yasuhito and Christie W. Kiefer. 1993. *Refuge of the Honored: Social Organization in a Japanese Retirement Community.* Berkeley: University of California Press.

Kitagawa, Evelyn M. and Philip M. Hauser. 1973. *Differential Mortality in the United States: A Study in Socioeconomic Epidemiology.* Cambridge, MA: Harvard University Press.

Klein, J. 1995. "AARP? ARRGH. Why Baby Boomers Should Reject the Senior Citizens' Lobby." *Newsweek,* May 15, p. 27.

Kohli, Martin, Martin Rein, Anne-Marie Guillemard, and Herman Van Gunsteren, eds. 1991. *Time for Retirement: Comparative Studies of Early Exit from the Labor Force.* Cambridge, UK: Cambridge University Press.

Korpi, Walter. 1983. *The Democratic Class Struggle.* London: Routledge and Kegan Paul.

Kotlikoff, Laurence J. 1992. *Generational Accounting: Knowing Who Pays, and When, for What We Spend.* New York: Free Press.

Koyano, W. 1989. "Japanese Attitudes toward the Elderly: A Review of Research Findings." *Journal of Cross-Cultural Gerontology* 4:335-45.

Kristof, N. D. 1996. "Aging World, New Wrinkles." *New York Times,* September 22, p. 4-1.

Kunst, A. E. and J. P. Mackenbach. 1994. "The Size of Mortality Differences Associated with Educational Level in Nine Industrialized Countries." *American Journal of Public Health* 84:932-37.

Langdon, D. 1982. "Claude Pepper, A Southern Gentleman with a Fist of Iron, Takes on the President to Defend the Elderly." *People,* June 21, pp. 38-41.

Langer, J. 1995. "Eight Boomers' Views." *American Demographics* 17(12):34-41.

Lanier, L. 1985. "A Longtime Pensioner." *U.S. News & World Report,* August 12, p. 42.

Laslett, Peter. 1971. *The World We Have Lost.* London: Routledge and Kegan Paul.

———. 1976. "Societal Development and Aging." Pp. 87-116 in *Handbook of Aging and the Social Sciences,* edited by Robert H. Binstock and Ethel Shanas. New York: Von Nostrand Reinhold.

———. 1991. *A Fresh Map of Life: The Emergence of the Third Age.* Cambridge, MA: Harvard University Press.

Lewis, J. 1992. "Gender and the Development of Welfare Regimes." *Journal of European Social Policy* 3:159-73.

Longman, Phillip. 1987. *Born to Pay: The New Politics of Aging in America.* Boston: Houghton Mifflin.

Lye, D. L. 1996. "Adult Child-Parent Relationships." *Annual Review of Sociology* 22:79-102.

Manton, K. G. 1982. "Temporal and Age Variation in the United States' Black-White Cause-Specific Mortality Differentials: A Study of the Recent Changes in the Relative Health Status of the United States Black Population." *The Gerontologist* 22:170-79.

———. 1990. "Mortality and Morbidity." Pp. 64-90 in *Handbook of Aging and the Social Sciences*. 3d ed., edited by Robert H. Binstock and Linda K. George. San Diego, CA: Academic Press.

Manton, K. G., E. Stallard, and L. Corder. 1995. "Changes in Morbidity and Chronic Disability in the U.S. Elderly Population: Evidence from the 1982, 1984, and 1989 National Long Term Care Surveys." *Journal of Gerontology: Social Sciences* 50B:S194-204.

Margolis, Richard J. 1990. *Risking Old Age in America*. Boulder, CO: Westview.

Markides, K., J. Liang, and J. S. Jackson. 1990. "Race, Ethnicity, and Aging: Conceptual and Methodological Issues." Pp. 112-129 in *Handbook of Aging and the Social Sciences*. 3d ed., edited by Robert H. Binstock and Linda K. George. San Diego, CA: Academic Press.

Markides, Kyriakos S. and Charles H. Mindel. 1987. *Aging and Ethnicity*. Newbury Park, CA: Sage.

Marmor, Theodore R., Jerry L. Mashaw, and Philip L. Harvey. 1990. *America's Misunderstood Welfare State: Persistent Myths, Enduring Realities*. New York: Basic Books.

Marshall, V. W., F. L. Cook, and J. G. Marshall. 1993. "Conflict over Intergenerational Equity: Rhetoric and Reality in a Comparative Context." Pp. 119-40 in *The Changing Contract across Generations*, edited by Vern L. Bengtson and W. Andrew Achenbaum. New York: Aldine de Gruyter.

McLaughlin, D. K. and L. Jensen. 1993. "Poverty among Older Americans: The Plight of Nonmetropolitan Elders." *Journal of Gerontology: Social Sciences* 48:S44-54.

Menchik, P. L. 1993. "Economic Status as a Determinant of Mortality among Black and White Older Men: Does Poverty Kill?" *Population Studies* 47:427-36.

Meyer, M. H. 1990. "Family Status and Poverty among Older Women: The Gendered Distribution of Retirement Income in the United States." *Social Problems* 37:1101-13.

Minkler, M. 1991. "'Generational Equity' and the New Victim Blaming." Pp. 67-80 in *Critical Perspectives on Aging: The Political and Moral Economy of Growing Old*, edited by Meredith Minkler and Carroll L. Estes. Amityville, NY: Baywood.

Moon, M. and P. Ruggles. 1994. "The Needy or Greedy? Assessing Income Support Needs of an Aging Population." Pp. 207-26 in *Economic Security and Intergenerational Justice: A Look at North America*, edited by Theodore R. Marmor, Timothy M. Smeeding, and Vernon L. Greene. Washington, DC: Urban Institute.

Moore, D. E. 1990. "Occupational Careers and Mortality of Elderly Men." *Demography* 27:31-53.

Morgan, S. P., and K. Hirosima. 1983. "The Persistence of Extended Family Residence in Japan: Anachronism or Alternative Strategy?" *American Sociological Review* 48:269-81.

Moseley, R. 1993. "Pension Sticker Shock in Europe: As More People Live Longer, Recession Is Threatening Benefits. *Chicago Tribune,* November 23, p. N-1.

Mott, F. L. and R. J. Haurin. 1985. "Factors Affecting Mortality in the Years Surrounding Retirement." Pp. 31-56 in *Retirement among American Men,* edited by Herbert S. Parnes, Joan E. Crowley, R. Jean Haurin, William R. Morgan, Frank L. Mott, and Gilbert Nestel. Lexington, MA: Lexington Books.

Mutchler, J. E., J. A. Burr, A. M. Pienta, and M. P. Massagli. 1997. "Pathways to Labor Force Exit: Work Transitions and Work Instability." *Journal of Gerontology: Social Sciences* 52B:S4-12.

Mutran, E. 1985. "Intergenerational Support among Blacks and Whites: Response to Cultural or Socioeconomic Differences." *Journal of Gerontology* 40:382-89.

Myerhoff, Barbara G. 1979. *Number Our Days.* New York: Simon and Schuster.

Myles, John. 1984. *Old Age in the Welfare State: The Political Economy of Public Pensions.* Boston: Little, Brown.

Myles, John and Jill Quadagno, eds. 1991. *States, Labor Markets, and the Future of Old Age Policy.* Philadelphia: Temple University Press.

———. 1994. "The Politics of Income Security for the Elderly in North America: Founding Cleavages and Unresolved Conflicts." Pp. 61-90 in *Economic Security and Intergenerational Justice: A Look at North America,* edited by Theodore R. Marmor, Timothy M. Smeeding, and Vernon L. Greene. Washington, DC: Urban Institute.

Nash, N. C. 1995. "Europeans Shrug as Taxes Go Up." *New York Times,* February 16, p. A-10.

Neugarten, Dial A., ed. 1996. *The Meaning of Age: Selected Papers of Bernice L. Neugarten.* Chicago: University of Chicago Press.

Ogawa, N. and R. D. Retherford. 1997. "Shifting Costs of Caring for the Elderly Back to Families in Japan: Will It Work?" *Population and Development Review* 23:59-94.

O'Higgins, M. 1988. "The Allocation of Public Resources to Children and the Elderly in OECD Countries." Pp. 201-28 in *The Vulnerable,* edited by John L. Palmer, Timothy Smeeding, and Barbara Boyle Torrey. Washington, DC: Urban Institute.

O'Rand, A. M. 1996. "The Precious and the Precocious: Understanding Cumulative Disadvantage and Cumulative Advantage over the Life Course." *The Gerontologist* 36:230-38.

Organization for Economic Cooperation and Development. 1988. *Reforming Public Pensions.* Paris: Organization for Economic Cooperation and Development.

―――. 1992. *Private Pensions and Public Policy.* Paris: Organization for Economic Cooperation and Development.

Orloff, A. S. 1993. "Gender and the Social Rights of Citizenship: The Comparative Analysis of Gender Relations and Welfare States." *American Sociological Review* 58:303-28.

Orloff, A. S. and T. Skocpol. 1984. "Why Not Equal Protection? Explaining the Politics of Public Social Spending in Britain, 1900-1911, and the United States, 1890s-1920." *American Sociological Review* 49:726-50.

Palme, Joakim. 1990. *Pension Rights in Welfare Capitalism: The Development of Old-Age Pensions in 18 OECD Countries, 1930 to 1985.* Stockholm: Swedish Institute for Social Research, University of Stockholm.

Palmore, Erdman, ed. 1984. *Handbook on the Aged in the United States.* Westport, CT: Greenwood.

―――. 1993. "Is Aging Really Better in Japan?" *The Gerontologist* 33:697-99.

Palmore, Erdman B., Bruce M. Burchett, Gerda G. Fillenbaum, Linda K. George, and Laurence M. Wallman. 1985. *Retirement: Causes and Consequences.* New York: Springer.

Palmore, Erdman B. and D. Maeda. 1985. *The Honorable Elders Revisited: A Revised Cross-Cultural Analysis of Aging in Japan.* Durham, NC: Duke University Press.

Pampel, F. C. 1994. "Population Aging, Class Context, and Age Inequality in Public Spending." *American Journal of Sociology* 100:153-95.

Pampel, F. C. and M. Hardy. 1994a. "Changes in Income Inequality During Old Age." *Research in Stratification and Mobility* 13:239-64.

―――. 1994b. "Status Maintenance and Change during Old Age." *Social Forces* 73:289-314.

Parker, M. G., M. Thorslund, and O. Lundberg. 1994. "Physical Function and Social Class among Swedish Oldest Old." *Journal of Gerontology: Social Sciences* 49:S196-201.

Parnes, H. S. and L. J. Less. 1985. "The Volume and Patterns of Retirement, 1966-1981." Pp. 91-118 in *Retirement among American Men,* edited by Herbert S. Parnes, Joan E. Crowley, R. Jean Haurin, William R. Morgan, Frank L. Mott, and Gilbert Nestel. Lexington, MA: Lexington Books.

Parsons, T. 1943. "The Kinship System of the Contemporary United States." *American Anthropologist* 45:22-38.

Pierson, P. and M. Smith. 1994. "Shifting Fortunes of the Elderly: The Comparative Politics of Retrenchment." Pp. 21-60 in *Economic Security and Intergenerational Justice: A Look at North America,* edited by Theodore R. Marmor, Timothy M. Smeeding, and Vernon L. Greene. Washington, DC: Urban Institute.

Piven, Francis Fox and Richard A. Cloward. 1982. *The New Class War.* New York: Pantheon.

Ponza, M., G. J. Duncan, M. Corcoran, and F. Groskind. 1988. "The Guns of Autumn? Age Differences in Support for Income Transfers to the Young and Old." *Public Opinion Quarterly* 52:492-512.

Preston, Samuel H. 1984. "Children and the Elderly: Divergent Paths for America's Dependents." *Demography* 21:435-58.

Quadagno, J. S. 1984. "Welfare Capitalism and the Social Security Act of 1935." *American Sociological Review* 49:632-47.

———. 1988. "Women's Access to Pensions and the Structure of Eligibility Rules." *Sociological Quarterly* 29:541-58.

———. 1989. "Generational Equity and the Politics of the Welfare State." *Politics & Society* 17:353-76.

———. 1996. "Social Security and the Myth of the Entitlement Crisis." *The Gerontologist* 36:391-99.

Quinn, J. F. 1987. "The Economic Status of the Elderly: Beware of the Mean." *Review of Income and Wealth* 33:63-82.

Quinn, J. F. and R. V. Burkhauser. 1990. "Work and Retirement." Pp. 308-27 in *Handbook of Aging and the Social Sciences.* 3d ed., edited by Robert H. Binstock and Linda K. George. San Diego, CA: Academic Press.

Rein, Martin and Lee Rainwater. 1986. *Public/Private Interplay in Social Protection: A Comparative Study.* Armonk, NY: M. E. Sharpe.

Rejda, George E. 1994. *Social Insurance and Economic Security.* 5th ed. Englewood Cliffs, NJ: Prentice Hall.

Reskin, Barbara and Irene Padavic. 1994. *Women and Men at Work.* Thousand Oaks, CA: Pine Forge Press.

Riley, Matilda White, Robert L. Kahn, and Anne Foner, eds. 1994. *Age and Structural Lag: Society's Failure to Provide Meaningful Opportunities in Work, Family, and Leisure.* New York: John Wiley.

Rimlinger, Gaston V. 1971. *Welfare Policy and Industrialization in Europe, America and Russia.* New York: John Wiley.

Rogers, R. G., R. A. Hummer, C. B. Nam, and K. Peters. 1996. "Demographic, Socioeconomic, and Behavioral Factors Affecting Ethnic Mortality by Cause." *Social Forces* 74:1419-38.

Rogers, R. G., A. Rogers, and A. Berlanger. 1992. "Disability-Free Life among the Elderly in the United States: Sociodemographic Correlates of Functional Health." *Journal of Aging and Health* 4:19-42.

Rollinson, P. A. 1990. "The Story of Edward: The Everyday Geography of Elderly Single-Room Occupancy (SRO) Hotel Tenants." *Journal of Contemporary Ethnography* 19:188-206.

Ross, C. E. and C. Wu. 1996. "Education, Age, and the Cumulative Advantage in Health." *Journal of Health and Social Behavior* 37:104-20.

Ruhm, C. J. 1990. "Bridge Jobs and Partial Retirement." *Journal of Labor Economics* 8:482-501.

Rushkoff, Douglas, ed. 1994. *The Gen X Reader.* New York: Ballantine.

Schulz, James H. 1980. *The Economics of Aging.* 2d ed. Belmont, CA: Wadsworth.

Shalev, M. 1983. "The Social Democratic Model and beyond: Two Generations of Comparative Research on the Welfare State." *Comparative Social Research* 6:315-52.

Shea, D. G., T. Miles, and M. D. Hayward. 1996. "The Health-Wealth Connection: Racial Differences." *The Gerontologist* 36:342-49.

Sheehy, Gail. 1995. *New Passages: Mapping Your Life across Time.* New York: Random House.

Silverstein, M. and L.J. Waite. 1993. "Are Blacks More Likely Than Whites to Receive and Provide Social Support in Middle and Old Age? Yes, No, and Maybe So?" *Journal of Gerontology: Social Sciences* 48:S212-22.

Skocpol, Theda. 1992. *Protecting Soldiers and Mothers: The Political Origins of Social Policy in the United States.* Cambridge, MA: Belknap.

———. 1995. *Social Policy in the United States: Future Possibilities in Historical Perspective.* Princeton, NJ: Princeton University Press.

Sloan, A. 1997. "Retirement Roulette." *Newsweek,* January 20, pp. 24-28.

Smeeding, T. M. 1990. "Economic Status of the Elderly." Pp. 362-81 in *Handbook of Aging and the Social Sciences.* 3d ed., edited by Robert H. Binstock and Linda K. George. San Diego, CA: Academic Press.

Smith, L. 1992. "The Tyranny of America's Old." *Fortune,* January 13, pp. 68-72.

Smith, R. 1961. "Japan: The Later Years of Life and the Concept of Time." Pp. 95-100 in *Aging and Leisure,* edited by R. Kleemeier. New York: Oxford University Press.

Smolensky, E., S. Danziger, and P. Gottschalk. 1988. "The Declining Significance of Age in the United States: Trends in the Well-Being of Children and the Elderly since 1939." Pp. 29-54 in *The Vulnerable,* edited by John L. Palmer, Timothy Smeeding, and Barbara Boyle Torrey. Washington, DC: Urban Institute.

Smolowe, J. 1992. "Where Children Come First." *Time,* November 9, p. 58.

Social Security Administration. 1985. *Social Security throughout the World.* Washington, DC: U.S. Government Printing Office.

South, S. 1991. "Age Structure and Public Expenditures on Children." *Social Science Quarterly* 72:661-75.

Stanford, E. Percil and Fernando M. Torres-Gil, eds. 1992. *Diversity: New Approaches to Ethnic Minority Aging.* Amityville, NY: Baywood.

Stephens, John D. 1986. *The Transition from Capitalism to Socialism.* Urbana: University of Illinois Press.

Stoller, Eleanor Palo and Rose Campbell Gibson, eds. 1994. *Worlds of Difference: Inequality in the Aging Experience.* Thousand Oaks, CA: Pine Forge Press.

Strauss, William and Neil Howe. 1991. *Generations: The History of America's Future, 1584 to 2069.* New York: Morrow.

Thomas, M. E., C. Herring, and H. D. Horton. 1994. "Discrimination over the Life-Course: A Synthetic Cohort Analysis of Earnings Differences between Black and White Males, 1940-1990." *Social Problems* 41:608-28.

Thomas, R. 1997. "Social Insecurity." *Newsweek,* January 20, pp. 21-23.

Thomma, S. 1997. "Where Do Your Tax Dollars Go?" *Boulder Daily Camera,* April 6, p. 4G.

Thomson, D. W. 1993. "A Lifetime of Privilege? Aging and Generations at Century's End." Pp. 215-38 in *The Changing Contract across Generations,* edited by Vern L. Bengtson and W. Andrew Achenbaum. New York: Aldine de Gruyter.

Thurow, Lester. 1996a. "The Elderly: America's New Revolutionary Class." *New York Times,* May 26, p. 46.

———. 1996b. *The Future of Capitalism.* New York: William Morrow.

Titmuss, Richard M. 1974. *Social Policy.* London: Allen and Unwin.

Torres-Gil, F. M. 1993. "Interest Group Politics: Generational Changes in the Politics of Aging." Pp. 239-58 in *The Changing Contract across Generations,* edited by Vern L. Bengtson and W. Andrew Achenbaum. New York: Aldine de Gruyter.

Tracy, M. and R. Ward. 1986. "Trends in Old Age Pensions for Women: Benefit Levels in Ten Nations, 1960-1980." *The Gerontologist* 26:286-91.

Uhlenberg, P. 1992. "Population Aging and Social Policy." *Annual Review of Sociology* 18:449-74.

U.S. Bureau of the Census. 1982. *Characteristics of Persons below the Poverty Line: 1982.* Current Population Reports, Series P60-144. Washington, DC: U.S. Government Printing Office.

———. 1992. *Poverty in the United States: 1992.* Current Population Reports, Series P60-185. Washington, DC: U.S. Government Printing Office.

———. 1994. *Statistical Abstract.* Washington, DC: U.S. Government Printing Office.

U.S. Senate, Special Committee on Aging. 1990. *Medicare Coverage of Catastrophic Health Care Costs: What Do Seniors Need, and What Do Seniors Want?* Washington, DC: U.S. Government Printing Office.

Vinovskis, M. A. 1993. "An Historical Perspective on Support for Schooling by Different Age Cohorts." Pp. 45-65 in *The Changing Contract across Generations,* edited by Vern L. Bengtson and W. Andrew Achenbaum. New York: Aldine de Gruyter.

Walker, A. 1993. "Intergenerational Relations and Welfare Restructuring: The Social Construction of an Intergenerational Problem." Pp. 141-66 in *The Changing Contract across Generations,* edited by Vern L. Bengtson and W. Andrew Achenbaum. New York: Aldine de Gruyter.

Wallace, S. P., J. B. Williamson, R. G. Lung, and L. A. Powell. 1988. "A Lamb in Wolf's Clothing? The Reality of Senior Power and Social Policy." Pp. 95-116 in *Critical Perspectives on Aging: The Political and Moral Economy of Growing Old*, edited by Meredith Minkler and Carroll L. Estes. Amityville, NY: Baywood.

Western, B. 1993. "Postwar Unionization in Eighteen Advanced Capitalist Countries." *American Sociological Review* 58:266-82.

Whiteford, P. 1995. "The Use of Replacement Rates in International Comparisons of Benefit Systems." *International Social Security Review* 48:3-29.

Wilensky, Harold L. 1975. *The Welfare State and Equality: Structural and Ideological Roots of Public Expenditures.* Berkeley: University of California Press.

Wisensale, S. K. 1988. "Generational Equity and Intergenerational Policies." *The Gerontologist* 28:773-78.

Williamson, John B., Linda Evans, and Lawrence A. Powell. 1982. *The Politics of Aging: Power and Policy.* Springfield, IL: Charles C Thomas.

Wolfson, M., G. Rowe, J. F. Gentleman, and M. Tomiak. 1993. "Career Earnings and Death: A Longitudinal Analysis of Older Canadian Men." *Journal of Gerontology: Social Sciences* 48:S167-79.

Yashiro, N. 1997. "The Economic Position of the Elderly." Pp. 89-110 in *The Economic Effects of Aging in the United States and Japan,* edited by Michael Hurd and Naohiro Yashiro. Chicago: University of Chicago Press.

Zsembik, B. A. and A. Singer. 1990. "The Problems of Defining Retirement among Minorities: The Mexican Americans." *The Gerontologist* 30:749-57.

Index

Organization for Economic
  Cooperation and Development
  (OECD), 107-108
Orloff, A. S., 121
Overgeneralizations, 3

Padavic, I., 88
Palme, J., 31, 100, 105, 111
Palmore, E. B., 64, 94, 112, 114
Pampel, F. C., 71, 145, 147
Parker, M. G., 66
Parnes, H. S., 63, 70
Parsons, T., 10
Pavalko, E. K., 63
Payroll taxes, 15
Pelham, A. O., 75, 79
Pension systems, public:
  conservative policy regime, 109
  inequality, 106-108
  Japan, 111-114
  liberal policy regime, 109-110
  outcome differences, 110-111
  rights, public pension,
    104-106
  rules for allotment of benefits,
    100-101
  social democratic policy regime,
    108-109
  See also Social Security
Peters, K., 85
Pienta, A. M., 62, 83
Pierson, P., 141
Piven, F. F., 116
Policies and old age, public, 25
  class differences, 71
  conclusions, 48-49
  double jeopardy, 80-81
  generations, inequality across age
    groups and, 133-135
  government social protection,
    26-29
  inequality, sources of, 41-45
  politics of inequality, 46-48

racial and ethnic groups, 78
support for public programs,
  36-41
welfare state, 30-36
See also Comparative perspective,
  old age support in
Politics:
  generational tensions, 148
  of inequality, 46-48
  power and increased aged
    population, 128, 137
Ponza, M., 137
Population figures for the elderly,
  14-15, 102, 127-130
Poverty rates/levels:
  charting trends, 4-5
  gender issues, 91, 92
  near-poor elderly, 8
  OECD statistics, 107-108
  racial and ethnic groups, 85-88
  Social Security, 6
  subgroups, 8
Powell, L. A., 137, 141
Preston, D. P., 21
Preston, S. H., 84, 127, 131
Private income, 9, 58-59, 71-72
Public programs assisting the elderly,
  3-6, 9, 89
  See also Policies and old age,
    public

Quadagno, J. S., 16, 90, 117, 135, 136,
  140, 141, 144
Quinn, J. F., 32, 45

Race, 22
Racial and ethnic groups:
  conclusions, 97
  discrimination, 74-75
  double jeopardy, 79-81
  familism, 91-97
  health status/issues, 83-85